CW00393359

GOOD MORNING, BABYLON

Good Morning, Babylon

PAOLO AND
VITTORIO TAVIANI

with the collaboration of
Tonino Guerra

from an idea by Lloyd Fouvielle

faber and faber
LONDON · BOSTON

First published in 1987
by Faber and Faber Limited
3 Queen Square London WC1N 3AU

Photoset by Wilmaset Birkenhead Wirral
Printed in Great Britain by
Redwood Burn Ltd Trowbridge Wiltshire
All rights reserved

British Library Cataloguing in Publication Data

Taviani, Paolo
Good morning, Babylon.
I. Title   II. Taviani, Vittorio
852'.914   PN1997.P233
ISBN 0–571–15065–9

This book would not have been possible without
the special assistance of Vanni Corbellini.

When we talk about Utopia, it's not just wishful thinking, imagining something that will never happen.

We mean that when a man has started to plan and make projects for the future, the mere fact that he's working at it is already something real and constructive.

We don't know whether his project will be fully realized. But we know that if a man today is working for tomorrow, then that influences his life and the lives of others.

That's what Utopia means to us.

Contents

ix

Brothers in Arms:
cinematic prisms and political spectrums in the work of Paolo and Vittorio Taviani

Premises, premises: California dreaming

When Rossellini imposed his presidential will on the 1977 Cannes Film Festival Jury and brought Paolo and Vittorio Taviani's *Padre, Padrone* to the attention of international markets, he was conscious of the responsibility of keeping alive a certain tradition of Italian cinema. As a benign, but determined, padre/padrone himself, he seemed to be taking out an insurance policy against future fads and fashions in the hope of stimulating dwindling interest in Italian neo-realism. Hitherto, he had looked on the progress of hard-hitting 'second wave' neo-realists like Pasolini and Bertolucci with considerable apprehension. The former's views on sexual politics, and his uncompromising, ideological stance against any form of *omologazione* of the sub-proletariat in the cauldron of Italy's economic 'miracle' in the 1960s, made him sceptical. As for Bertolucci, the early promise of *La Commare Secca* (*The Grim Reaper*, 1962) and *Prima della Rivoluzione* (*Before the Revolution*, 1964) seemed to him little more than polite acknowledgements before a passionate affair with another 'wayward' son: Jean-Luc Godard.

Most of the other 'serious' directors who continued to believe in the precepts of neo-realism, way beyond its 'official' death at the Parma Congress of 1954, were better intentioned but far less talented. Rossellini had turned to television for money and to the Directorship of the Centro Sperimentale (the Italian film school) for continuing influence and power. The fact that *Padre, Padrone* had been financed by RAI-TV as part of a systematic intervention in production and that his own most recent films *Il Messia* (*The Messiah*, 1976) and *Italia, Anno Uno* (*Italy, Year One*, 1976) had also been completed by means of similar arrangements with RAI, helped to strengthen the case.

I

Those he could not persuade by rational argument, he seduced; those he could not seduce, he exhausted with his legendary stubbornness. The walls of the Carlton Hotel in Cannes still resound with an accumulation of anecdotes and rumours about one of the most memorable confrontations of the last ten years. So much so that Gilles Jacob, the Director of the Festival, thought it best to 'sign up' the Tavianis' new film for the official section (but out of competition) for the 1987 edition while *Good Morning, Babylon* was still a mirage in their collective eyes.

What was at stake was far more than Rossellini's prestige, or even the sharpness of his political (as well as aesthetic) judgement. What was at stake was an *idea* of cinema which had proved to be the only real alternative to the Hollywood machine since the birth of the 'talkies'.

In that context *Good Morning, Babylon* is set to become a milestone in the history of the cinema, since no major Italian director worthy of his cinematic salt, with the exception of Michelangelo Antonioni and, to some extent, Sergio Leone, has ever dared to venture into the hallowed halls of Hollywood's studios, and what is more with a subject that digs deep into the roots of American imagination on the largest possible screen.

If Rossellini had kidnapped Ingrid Bergman, generating one of the most vicious smear campaigns ever mounted by the powerful hacks of America's gutter press, the Tavianis' trajectory brought them straight to the heart of Hollywood mythology: D. W. Griffith's legendary and misunderstood *Intolerance*.

Significantly, the film is set at a time in which the constitution of Hollywood's cinematic conventions was still being established. Epics, melodramas and Westerns dominated the production schedules of the independents who had successfully dismantled the apparatus of Edison's Motion Picture Patents Company. The hegemony of a wider variety of genres (musicals, gangster films, social and screwball comedies) established with the coming of sound in the late 1920s and 30s had yet to destabilize the European film industry.

In fact, Italian companies like Cines in Rome, Anonima Ambrosio and Italia Films in Turin and Luca Comerio in Milan, with their lavish epics, had been at the forefront of a substantial assault on the American market since 1908. D. W. Griffith himself on many occasions had expressed his admiration and his debt to films by Giovanni Pastrone (alias Piero Fosco) like *La Caduta di Troia* (1912) and the famous *Cabiria* (1913–14) with the collaboration of Gabriele D'Annunzio; by Enrico Guazzoni like *Quo Vadis?* (1913); by Mario Caserini like *Parsifal e Sigfrido* (1912) and *Gli Ultimi Giorni di Pompei* (1913); by actor/director Guiseppe De Liguoro like *Odissea* and *Inferno* (both 1912) drawn from Dante Alighieri's *La Divina Commedia*.

So the Tavianis' project comes full circle. Based on the true story of three Italian carpenters (or rather 'cathedral builders and restorers'), responsible for setting up an impressive exhibition of stage sets as part of the 1914 San Francisco Exposition, *Good Morning, Babylon* traces their brilliant careers (significantly the three have shrunk to two) after being signed up by none other than Mr Griffith himself. With Ed Pressman as their American mentor the Tavianis' own future might, eventually, follow the trajectory traced by their protagonists, Andrea and Nicola Bonanno.

But the Tavianis are keen to stress that *Good Morning, Babylon* is not a film *about* America, since they do not feel qualified to attempt such a (dangerous) venture:

It's a film about two artisans who realize that their training in designing and constructing Romanesque cathedrals and monumental buildings, in the twentieth century, is viable only in the context of the playground that is the cinema. Building a cathedral and making a movie are similar processes and if D. W. Griffith's films are *about* history, they also *become* history.

The notion of complicity that springs from this description is free from any association with a sense of nostalgia or false sentimentalism. Its roots are to be found in the ideological commitment the two brothers have to the representation of history through the principles signalled by Michel Foucault and others in the formulation of a 'popular memory'.

Neo-real landscapes

In order to understand this more fully it is necessary to take a step back and attempt to place the Tavianis' work in the texture of Italian cinema and, above all, Italian society. Taking a step back in matters relating to Italian cinema means, inevitably, bumping into Rossellini again, conscious of the creed expressed by the inveterate cinephile of Bertolucci's *Prima della Rivoluzione*: 'I saw *Viaggio in Italia* ten times . . . Remember, you cannot *live* without Rossellini!'

Although Rossellini was firmly established within the ranks of the ruling Christian Democrat party, his allegiances in the world of cinema were determined by his anti-sectarian 'vision'. His endorsement of the Tavianis' cinema was part of a process of integration and cross-fertilization which was rendered complete by the release of *Padre, Padrone* in the Christian Democrat-controlled private exhibition circuit, and the acquisition of Rossellini's *Story of Christ (Il Messia)* by the rival Communist-based network ARCI. This may already indicate the difficulties (and the necessity) of placing the Tavianis' films in the complexities of the Italian political spectrum. It also stresses the need to take into consideration the precise historical moment and conditions of each production.

To begin with, Paolo and Vittorio's middle-class, Tuscan background – Paolo was born in 1931, Vittorio in 1929, in San Miniato (more clearly in evidence in *The Night of San Lorenzo* than anywhere else before *Good Morning, Babylon*) must be weighed against four important sets of relationships:

1. The theatre (more available to them in the small town of San Miniato, not far geographically from Florence – but a world apart in terms of taste and people) and music (both become accomplished musicians early on) as preparation for their move to the Cinema City that is Rome.
2. The influence of neo-realism in the form of *Paisa* and early Visconti, seen as a rejection of the naturalist strains developed by the more adventurous directors of the 1930s in Italy, and as an encouragement to work in the cinema. Their apprenticeship as assistant directors with such as Biagetti,

Pellegrini, Nelli, Bragaglia and, of course, Rossellini provides them with an idea of what to aim for as well as what to leave behind, without regrets.

3. The meeting with trade-unionist film-maker Valentino Orsini, with whom they are to make their first twelve films from 1954 to 1963, and the move from documentary through Joris Ivens to fiction.

4. The meeting with Giuliani G. De Negri who becomes more than their producer for all their features from *Un Uomo Da Bruciare* (1962) through to *Good Morning, Babylon*.

Significantly their first short is a collaboration with the 'instinctual' cornerstone of 'classical' neo-realism, Cesare Zavattini, set at the time of Mussolini's last stand with the Salò Republic and centred on the experiences of their fellow townsfolk: *San Miniato, 1944*. This is a text-book *hommage* to neo-real fathers but, after the cathartic encounter with Joris Ivens at the time of *L'Italia non e' un Paese Povero* (1960), and the realization that the interface between 'documentary' and 'neo-realism' is rather slippery, they decide to shift towards the other side of the neo-realist equation and plunge into the aesthetics of fiction.

At first, the mediating influence of Valentino Orsini allowed the transition to occur smoothly *Un Uomo Da Bruciare* (1962), their first fiction feature, contains all the key narrative elements which will become the 'auteurist' signature of the Taviani brothers. The return of Salvatore to his native Sicily predates Fulvio's troubled journey south in *Allonsanfan* (1974) and the Tavianis' own return in *Xaos* (1984) and their Sardinian equivalent in *Padre, Padrone* (1977). Salvatore's attempts at consciousness-raising and the organization of the peasants, thwarted and eventually destroyed by the Mafia, opens with a song in which he sings solo to the peasants' forceful chorus. His function is that of a 'sacrificial lamb' who, like Fulvio and Giulio in *San Michele Aveva un Gallo* (1971), will never be able to fully realize his ideals and yet is incapable of blending into the stubborn, 'secular' force of the collectivity and their almost mechanical refrain. The parable-like structure of the film provides the film-makers with a series of tableaux that will help them to fix the method by which they will, in future, attempt to articulate their ideological soul-searching.

As they do so, however, the partnership with Valentino Orsini begins to loosen. The crisis point and the consequent break comes with the film *I Fuorilegge Del Matrimonio* (1963), commissioned to explore attitudes towards divorce, the law and especially the piece of legislation known by the name of its instigator as the Sansone Bill (1953). Like Pasolini's documentary on changing sexual mores (*Comizi D'Amore*) a few years later, the Tavianis' film incurs the wrath of the ruling Christian Democrats and the religious establishment. This results, perhaps indirectly, in their (and Orsini's) inability to raise finance for any project for the following five years.

At this point it may be well to consider the place of neo-realism in the Tavianis' broader allegiance to what they see as the 'continuity of the most authentic strand in Italian Culture'. In an interview in 1969 (*Cinema e Film*, No. 7–8, winter–spring 1969), the two authors discuss their relation to Pirandello, Verdi, Michelangelo and Machiavelli, picking out themes and motifs from all the arts, but especially from music, to support an idea of cinematic *Gesamtkunstwerk*, capable of containing materialist readings of 'social fictions'. Musical structures and the tradition of the 'Melodramma' are the models invoked in what they call their search for the 'spirituality of politics . . . it is our way of looking for God; as atheists do, of course' (*Cahiers Du Cinema*, No. 228, March–April 1971). Their approach to music is symptomatic of this search: 'We feel that our films are closer to music than to literature in the way that Visconti was close to literature and Pasolini to painting, for instance' (*La Repubblica* Wed., 3 August 1983) and again: 'Music is fundamental to us not as a form of commentary as it is normally employed in the cinema, but as an element with equal weight and equal status as an image, as a character.' (*Cinema sessanta* No. 116, July–August 1977).

The central issue thus becomes the orchestration of opposing forces seen in terms of Brechtian 'gestures': the struggle of the individual and the struggle of the masses; the anarchy of imagination and 'action' opposed to the rational delineation of a party programme; the symbiosis of leadership and treason; the function of martyrdom and the determinations of (self) sacrifice; the representation of history as a moral (fairy) tale.

In the immediate pre-'68 climate, it is the lesson of Communist Party, Gramscian intellectual Franco Fortini (*Verifica dei Poteri*, 1965) and the debate about the social mandate of artists and writers that tempers the impulses of neo-realist partisanship for the Taviani brothers. In *Sovversivi* (1968) the funeral of Communist Party leader Palmiro Togliatti and the symbolic burial of the last vestiges of neo-realism are the Tavianis' answer to Marco Bellocchio's *Fists in the Pocket* and Bernardo Bertolucci's *Before The Revolution*. The five stories concerning a cross-section of Italian life already prefigure the sense of post-'68 depression and involution soon to grip most of their more famous contemporaries. Bertolucci's *Partner* is perhaps the best example of the emergence of a feeling of confused impotence, while Bellocchio's inability to bury the ghost of his icon, Lou Castel, until *The Eyes The Mouth* (1982) is the symptom of a widespread, contagious disease which the Tavianis, by identifying it earlier, are able to vaccinate themselves against, to the horror of many.

Ludovico, the paralysed film-maker unable to work on a project about Leonardo, serves as a prophetic metaphor for the general disillusionment which is to follow the triumphant entrance into film of the various Maoist and extra-parliamentary groups. It is precisely in this context that the Tavianis' first film without the 'reassuring' presence of Valentino Orsini is subjected to a barrage of attacks and charges of defeatism. The most vociferous opponent is the *intellettuale d'assalto*, Goffredo Fofi, whose legendary magazine, *Ombre Rosse* (literally 'Red Shadows', but rendered ambivalent by the fact that it was the Italian title for John Ford's *Stagecoach*) is the bastion of the revolution for student radicals and politicized film-makers alike. Branded the 'misguided, blind kittens of the revolution', the Taviani brothers contend that they want to make behaviourist and not ideological films (*sic*), that the 'subversive' of the title is an adjective to indicate an 'attitude, by which the present needs to be accepted completely but only in order to verify it, to contradict it'.

Isolated, but very much part of the debates, Paolo and Vittorio Taviani reach 1968 with renewed determination and the conviction of an 'autonomous' style. *Sotto Il Segno Dello Scorpione* (1969) marks the definitive break with a certain neo-realist orthodoxy (buried but not exorcized in their previous film), and develops their growing concern for formal and aesthetic ambivalence. The sign of the scorpion of the title is the October Revolution, poised to commit suicide when encircled by the fire of history, and desperately seeking a piece of *terra firma* in the chaos and confusion of the times. It is a parable set outside time, on a symbolic island; a metaphorical present without the analytical strengths of Pasolini's *Pigsty* (so similar in other respects). A difficult and intriguing film, without the narrative sophistication of the later work, it functions as a self-conscious discussion of their narrative method rather than in the fully fledged, conventional style which marks their commercially more successful films of the 1970s. The symbols are clearly set in opposition, with particular attention paid to an internal dynamism rather than narrative coherence. Significantly, it is shortly after this film's release that the brothers are able to articulate in interviews, for the first time, their relationship with Rossellini's neo-realism: 'It is a love–hate relationship like that of a father to a son. Born from a father we loved and admired, we have come to deny him with all the violence that a child may draw upon to assert himself and rejoice at the destruction of his parent . . .'

For veteran critic Guido Aristarco, whose dogmatic, entrenched magazine *Cinema Nuovo* had always tried to defend the Tavianis' work, somewhat 'against the grain', the key issue in relation to them *vis-à-vis* Rossellini was less bloody: 'The important feature of the Tavianis' work is the passage from chronicle to history. Rossellini is deeply convinced of his vision of history, but it's a vision tinged by mysticism. Rossellini mystifies and clouds over a notion of history in *Il Generale della Rovere* which he manages to avoid in *Paisa* and *Rome Open City* even though, by showing a priest helping the Resistance, he chooses to disregard the fact that the Vatican was actually on the side of the Germans right up to the last moment.' (*Cinema 73* No. 177, June 1973) Interestingly enough, this is the first Taviani film to catch the attention of *Cahiers du Cinema* and Pascal Kane's article ('Sous Le Signe du Scorpion' CDC Nos. 228 and 230, 1971), identifying the deterministic course of conflict within and without their films was later 'fleshed out' by a magazine formed by a break-away group of critics from *Cinema Nuovo* who dedicated their first issue to the Tavianis (*Cinema e Cinema* vol. 1 No. 1 Oct–Dec, 1974).

With *San Michele Aveva un Gallo* (1971), the two brothers consolidate, with official RAI-TV subsidy, their distinctive approach by emphasizing ambivalence in their visual and thematic motifs. At the end there are two boats: in one, the protagonist (Giulio) is being transferred from one prison to another, having questioned his past throughout the film in an isolated cell; in the other, a group of young revolutionaries in a parallel voyage poke fun at the intellectual and eventually lead him to suicide by drowning. This sequence represents the Tavianis' cinema in a nutshell. On the other hand, the Utopia of the radical intellectual, alone by definition, in love with a notion of self-sacrifice and destruction; on the other, the group of political realists, of 'socialist scientists' adept at bureaucratic organization. The tension is between a fervour for revolution at all costs, with a sense of 'nostalgia for the future', and the pessimism of reason sharpened by the constant reassessment of strategic necessities. Again the Tavianis resort to music to describe their formal design, which is based on the notion of a quartet. Paolo Taviani claims the influence of Stawinski in the structural and geographic dislocation of four main 'players' and four 'playing areas'. Fulvio Accialini and Lucia Coluccelli, authors of the first substantial book on the Tavianis (La Nuova Italia, 1979) add Beethoven (a frequent reference point for the brothers) and Brahms. But the majority of Italian critics show a great deal of indifference for these 'structuralist justifications' and from both the Left and the Right come some of the most aggressive rounds of critical fire. On the far left, *Il Manifesto* calls it a treason against everything which the Tavianis were assumed to uphold in identifying with at least a part of the revolutionary left of 1968. The PCI and the official film-makers of the party admire their style and rigour, but fail to engage fully with the 'message'. The right focuses its attack on the 'perversion' of the Tolstoyan matrix for the project.

Their next film *Allonsanfan* (1974) extends these oppositions and conflicts, and shows the same kind of organic intellectual being stoned to death by the uncomprehending masses who had already

9

sided with the soldiers in *San Michele*. The complexity of the central, aristocratic ex-would-be-revolutionary figure of Fulvio at the turn of the century is a sign of artistic maturity. The theme of actual versus suspected or strategic 'betrayals' provides a texture of narrative suspense which fully realizes the ambitions of films like *Sotto Il Segno Dello Scorpione* and *San Michele*. Their heretical obsession with the tragedy of the romantic hero, and their refusal to engage with contemporary issues in any but the most oblique, allegorical and pessimistic way, has been explained by the Tavianis as: 'The way to free ourselves of all illusions . . . repression on this part of us generates paralysis . . . only by freeing ourselves would we acquire the right to repropose a Utopia as a moment of truth, as a concrete plan for the future, to hope, in other words, for what may appear hopeless.' (*Cinema e Film* No. 1, 1974).

But it is with *Padre, Padrone* (1977) that most of the fiery polemics are resolved, at least on the sandy surface of the Croisette. The displacement of the central conflict from the analysis of historical/fictional moments of defeat on to the father–son relationship in a deprived, isolated part of Italy such as Sardinia seemed finally to make the Tavianis' work acceptable to everybody. All the ideological anxieties and ambiguities could be construed by the critics, now, as 'preparations' for the Oedipal resolution. Moreover, the presence of Gavino Ledda (the author of the book on which the film is based) serves as a delimitation of the fictional universe, allowing a certain distance from the vision of the parricide; a parricide endorsed so forcefully by the father of 'modern' Italian cinema: Roberto Rossellini.

Light at the end of the ideological tunnel

In this perspective it is not perhaps too surprising to find the Tavianis' films populated by children. As Accialini and Coluccelli point out (*op cit.* p. 98) 'seeing things through children's eyes' is a recurring motif in their work: the two brothers in *I Fuorilegge*; Muzio's son in *I Sovversivi*; the girl in *San Michele* who recounts the execution; Fulvio and Esther's offspring in *Allonsanfan*;

Gavino in the field of *Padre, Padrone*, of course; all the way up to the 'seven mouths to feed' in *Good Morning, Babylon*. Childhood is never seen as peaceful or sentimental, as Ermanno says in *I Sovversivi*: 'I will never allow anyone to say it is the best time of our lives.'

Something of the 'epic' quality of this vision of discovery into adulthood carries the Tavianis over their most underrated and misunderstood film: *Il Prato* (1979) starring Isabella Rossellini, Saverio Marconi and Michele Placido. The structure of this film is the perfect embodiment of their creed: 'The true autonomy of a work of art is the expression of clarity through simplicity' ('Linguaggio e Ideologia del Cinema', a paper delivered at the Pesaro Film Festival in 1967, published in Nuovi Quaderni, Parma, 1974). Essentially, *Il Prato* tells of the return of a youth to the countryside ('where nature weds history'). Like his counterparts in *Padre, Padrone* he discovers that this paradise on earth is unbearable and after grave doubts and torment he allows himself to die. The main female character (Isabella Rossellini is most certainly not a 'random choice') is much stronger than any other woman in their films up to that point. She holds the key to the 'fairy-tale' world that *The Night of San Lorenzo* will play on, and shuttles constantly back and forth between the various symbolic levels of the narrative, holding firmly on to the values transmitted to her by the children, the friends and the peasants that the young man is attempting to be part of. The ideological issues, always foregrounded up to this point, recede into the background of their formal search into a cinematic language of their own, displacing and angering some of the critics who had finally 'come round' to *Padre, Padrone*.

Yet it is one of their films closest to the contemporary world, to an image of the contradictions that govern a way of life that Italians have become accustomed to and seldom want to explore in such a direct manner. As Pietro Troesca points out in *Cinema e Utopia* (Nuovi Quaderni, San Gimignano, 1979) the 'negative hero [so often at the centre of the Tavianis' work – ed.] here becomes the heroism of pessimism, the patience to accept a given state of affairs'. From another angle, it is the dividing line between the 'chorus' and the leader as in *Un Uomo Da Bruciare* and *Allonsanfan*. These two poles are finally united in a character that rejects the matrix of the 'leader', forced upon so many of their earlier protagonists, and yet cannot find peace in the sense of belonging to the resigned mass. His own suicide is a disavowal, not a sacrifice. There is no redemption, no mocking Utopias to contend with, anymore.

From the brooding, linguistic and cinephile treatise of *Il Prato*, the Tavianis emerge with one of their most beautiful and least pessimistic works: *The Night of San Lorenzo* – a coming home that propelled them into the realm of the 'great Italian directors' beyond the shadow of a critic's doubt. Chronicle and History are joined finally in the epiphany of a truly epic vision, where the collectivity of a Tuscan village (San Martino, not unlike San Miniato . . .) under the occupation finds the strength to defy the command to congregate in their cathedral and sets off in search of their freedom. The caravan of men, women and children travel through geographical and ideological land mines with an almost spiritual sense of determination and purpose. Their hopes and anxieties are tied together by the magic of the 9th of August (the night of San Lorenzo) when the cascade of shooting stars points the way to the realization of the collective dream. Based on real characters and events, the film is 'narrated' by a six-year-old girl who interprets events, and papers over the cracks that emerge over forty years of story-telling, some of which has deep autobiographical roots for the two brothers. The narrative texture and the range of characters that populate this moving and accomplished film are impossible to analyse in any detail here. It is important, however, to point out that *The Night of San Lorenzo* marks the entrance of hope and a truly remarkable, if unexpected, 'rebirth of wonder', without which *Good Morning, Babylon* would have been inconceivable.

Between *The Night of San Lorenzo* and *Good Morning, Babylon* lies an episodic film, *Xaos* (1984), drawn from some of Pirandello's most significant short stories and instigated by RAI-TV. The scene set for its world première was the Venice Biennale and like Cannes seven years earlier, a festival became a turning point in their careers.

Having recovered its old knack for controversy the previous

year with an out-and-out war between the jury and the Italian critics over the merits of the Golden Lion Award (Jean-Luc Godard's *Prénom Carmen*), the Biennale of 1984 was in severe danger of falling apart thanks to the politically motivated machinations of director Gian Luigi Rondi, whose selection of films in competition left a lot to be desired. All the four Italian films he chose were appalling and one, Pasquale Squitieri's biography of Benito Mussolini's companion Claretta Petacci, starring his wife Claudia Cardinale, was received as a thinly disguised eulogy for fascist Italy. The art deco(ed) but austere press conference room turned into a rowdy fish market – in the best tradition of the Commedia All'Italiana. Spearheaded by Soviet poet Yevgeny Yevtushenko, jury members Rafael Alberti, Günter Grass and Erland Josephson were all bent on resigning from their duties. At one point, they came up with a suggestion strongly applauded by the critics: 'Throw the Taviani brothers off the jury for "bad conduct", so that then they would be able to award the main prize to their wonderful *Xaos*, which has had to be shown out of competition.' Chaos indeed. Somehow the Taviani brothers were placed in a position of simultaneously defending the place of Italian cinema in the Mostra as jury members and condemning it to the depths of hell through their magnificent work as film-makers. They managed, somehow, to hold the jury together, thus achieving a personal triumph on all fronts to the sheer delight of the Italian press.

This dual role gave them a long overdue place at the centre of Italian film culture. Everyone finally recognized how consistent and coherent they had been in their choices; how they had never courted the kind of favour that allegiance to the right party at the right time can provide in a country like Italy; how they had preferred to tread a careful path between such antinomies as History and Nature, Instinct and Reason, Rossellian *métier* and Pasolinian themes. In short, they became, overnight, the 'official' two-headed spokesperson for Italian cinema. And they speak as they direct: each answering in turn, frequently refining and sharpening the other's previous comment, and very seldom disagreeing with one another: 'Whatever recognition we have won abroad – as well as the success of films like Ermanno Olmi's *Tree of Wooden Clogs* or of Angelopoulos' work as a whole – proves that the best way to achieve a universal response is to be faithful to your own roots; to what you know best and what you care about most.' The principle of a cinema with deep roots in the earth of tradition is one they share with directors as diverse as Dovzhenko and Vidor, Tarkovsky and Huston, Ivens and Cavalcanti. It also provides the guiding principle for the selection of tales from Pirandello in *Xaos*:

> We deliberately chose stories that had ties to ancient Sicilian peasant folklore rather than the more intellectual and cosmopolitan ones, where you find his ridiculing of the middle classes and the moralistic aphorisms for which the author is best known, especially outside Italy.

But there were other reasons:

> After all, we made our first film (*Un Uomo Da Bruciare*) in Sicily, and felt that with this project we could pick up the threads of *Padre, Padrone* and continue to investigate the terms that define the relationship between man and nature – the dignity of man, his struggle, his piety in the cauldron of myth and peasant culture.

The major difference between *Xaos* and *Padre, Padrone*, however, is a stylistic one, largely attributable to the collaboration with director of photography Giuseppe Lanci (who made *Nostalghia* for Tarkovsky, just before) and the decision to make a nocturnal, predominantly 'lunar' film as opposed to the greater ideological clarity of *Padre, Padrone*:

> Our love for Pirandello predates that for Brecht and we were very conscious of not misrepresenting him. If anything, we wished to enter into a dialectical relationship in so far as, for him, the adventure of life is a constant struggle of which he knows only the outcome, which is silence. To us, precisely because of that struggle, the conclusions that may be drawn do not necessarily result in the tragedy of silence.

To an Italian audience, the film's most unexpected aspect is the use of two popular comic actors, Franco Franchi and Ciccio Ingrassia who, in something like one hundred and twenty comedies, had never been called upon to walk and chew gum at the same time.

It was important to us to respond to their deep Sicilian roots. They are two of the best-known actors in Italy and represent something that comes out in *La Giara* which is so quintessentially Sicilian. *La Giara* is the most famous of Pirandello's short stories, and because of that we thought very carefully about whether we should put it in at all. Then, very early on, we decided we had to make it with Franchi and Ingrassia, bringing out the dark side of Franchi's character – a sort of peasant mystic whose power to mend jars with his special glue is revered by the community, with a certain trepidation. People have commented on the great 'control' we exercised in this episode, and some were surprised to see a leitmotif of our previous films coming up here [the dance around the jar at night, echoing *Allonsanfan* in particular – ed.]. But we feel that the same considerations run through the film as a whole and not just this episode.

Xaos may bear a superficial relation to their only previous episodic film *Sovversivi*, but it is clearly not related to the popular compilation films of the 1960s, or to Pasolini's literary tales of the 1970s. And neither is it a convenient device to exploit Pirandello, to make a 'flexible' product which can accommodate the exigencies of television (four or five episodes, to which another couple can be tagged on if the going is good . . .)

We feel that the distinction between films made for TV and for the cinema is totally spurious. Television invests in films in various countries. We have made a film which could be shown in one sitting in normal theatrical circuits, and then could also be cut into two distinct parts for television programming. It's rather like the way they used to break films in the middle in the old days to allow you to sell ice-cream and pop corn.

On the crest of the Venetian waves, the Taviani brothers announced their new and most ambitious project to date: *Good Morning, Babylon*. The Babylon of the title recalls Kenneth Angers's kitsch description of Hollywood:

A mare's nest mountain of scaffolding, hanging gardens,

chariot-race ramparts and sky-high elephants, a make-believe mirage of Mesopotamia dropped down on the sleepy huddle of mission-style bungalows amid the orange groves that made up 1915 Hollywood, portent of things to come.

In describing thus the set of David Wark Griffith's *Intolerance*, Anger takes it as the sumptuous 'purple dawn' symbol of all Hollywood's dream machines. The original idea for the film, however, came from Lloyd Fouvielle in a two-page outline passed on to the Tavianis and Ed Pressman. The three script-writers (veteran Tonino Guerra joined Paolo and Vittorio from the beginning) decided early on to drop one of the 'real life' characters in favour of the symmetry afforded by two brothers in their mid-twenties who decide to seek the necessary funds to sustain their business at home and provide a livelihood for their five remaining brothers and their ageing father. But, they insist, there is no autobiography in the film:

> If anything we would rather see it as a biography of D. W. Griffith, who is a character we have always been fascinated by and whose courage we admire. The emphasis we would like to place is on the fact that two craftsmen *have to* emigrate in order to exercise their craft and to that extent it is also a film about Italy at that time.

But where, in Italy, the Bonanno brothers worked very much on the real surfaces of daily life, in town centres and harmonious piazzas, in America the job at hand is that of creating fantasies that will survive only in the minds of movie audiences. Ironically the massive reconstruction of D. W. Griffith's set on the 40-metre-square site in Tarquinia (courtesy of Carlo Ponti) is the reconstruction of a reconstruction of an imaginary world which the Bonannos intended to exploit in order to go back to building the 'real thing'. But they can't go home again:

> They discover that the dream of the cathedral, the myth of their craft which they imagine has been handed down to them through their ancestors all the way back to Giunta Pisano – the thirteenth-century expert of Romanesque cathedrals – is, in the twentieth century, the dream of the cinema. The encounter with Mr Griffith is the encounter

with a whole community of pioneers from all over the world, discovering together the magnificence of great new world.

If America is the dream, then the American Dream is the cinema of D. W. Griffith. Yet, although their father joins them in America as they are about to get married, he says to them: 'I have come, but I will not bless you because you have not kept your promise. You did not come back to continue your work.'

It is up to Mr Griffith to intervene at this point:

> I do not know whether our work, that of your sons and mine, is as fine as that of those who built the Romanesque cathedrals. I know that those works were born as these are born today – of the same collective dream, cultivated with humility and pride.
>
> I believe that your sons, Bonanno, are like those obscure stone-cutters who carved their masterpieces on the cathedrals you honour, who contributed to making them famous with their art, and who helped their neighbour to believe and live better.

So, in this sense, the film can be seen to attempt to build a bridge between the past and the present; between the old and the new; between the subliminal and the ephemeral; between European culture and American dreams. It is a unique adventure that brings the Taviani brothers, finally guiltless, into the blinding clarity of true spectacle. Not satisfied with reaching for the stars in *The Night of San Lorenzo*, they now land on the moon, having shed the overtly ideological constraints that were the 'sign of the scorpion' of post-'68. That is not to say, however, that they have abandoned all that, simply that they have passed through it and that they can now aspire to tell stories with the confidence of space travellers whose cultural and ideological roots are firmly planted in the fertile, ancient and noble land of self-questioning and doubt. As Pasolini's crow in *Uccellacci e Uccellini* (1966) would say: 'I come from the land of "laggiu", my father is ideology, my mother is doubt.' Here the crow has found an ally, in the shape of an elephant which towers above the Babylonian madness throughout the film.

The two-headed team splits for a second and it is Vittorio who explains:

There is an objective fact: there are elephants carved on the walls of Romanesque cathedrals and there are elephants that dominate Griffith's scenographies. What could that mean? Perhaps the continuity of mankind – so able, so thirsty to build and to create – can be symbolized by this animal with a proverbial memory, with extraordinary strength and with endless patience. It knows the secret that has prevented its extinction and that has preserved it from prehistoric time until today. In our film, it is not by chance that we never see an elephant lying down!

Mr Griffith would have been proud. So, come to think of it, would Michel Foucault.

Don Ranvaud

GOOD MORNING, BABYLON

The première of *Good Morning, Babylon,* a film by Paolo and Vittorio Taviani, took place at the Lumière cinema, London, on 28 August 1987.
The cast included:

Vincent Spano as NICOLA
Joaquim de Almeida as ANDREA
Greta Scacchi as EDNA
Desirée Becker as MABEL
Charles Dance as D. W. GRIFFITH

Directed by Paolo and Vittorio Taviani
Produced by Guiliani G. de Negri
Executive Producer   Edward Pressman
Art Director   Gianni Sbarra
Costumes   Lina Nerli Taviani
Editor   Roberto Perpignani
Director of Photography   Giuseppe Lanci (AIC)
Music   Nicola Piovani

1. EXT. CATHEDRAL. DAY

The side wall of a medieval cathedral fills the screen. The image is washed with sunlight. Into the frame steps BONANNO, *the old master builder. He slowly backs up, spreads his arms wide, and issues a command.*

BONANNO: Take down the scaffolding!

2. EXT. CATHEDRAL. DAY

The façade of the Romanesque Cathedral of San Michele, hidden behind scaffolding and sackcloth. On the scaffold and ladders bustle a swarm of artisans and workmen who are finishing the restoration work. Muscular arms grab hold of the huge structure of the scaffolding and start pulling it away from the cathedral. The ladders reaching to the top of the church are pulled to the ground. Sacks are ripped off, revealing the restored façade. Finally, the façade is free from its framework and drapery. The only thing still covered with a drape is the frieze over the central door. The old master builder impatiently waves his hand, ordering it to be removed.

BONANNO: And that one?

> *(The drapery is ripped off, revealing* ANDREA *and* NICOLA *giving the final touch to their part of the restoration: a bas-relief of a big white elephant standing on its hind legs with its trunk raised.)*

Andrea! Nicola!

> *(The two brothers wave cheerfully to their father as though to say, 'It's done. We're coming.' Their father squints to see better and smiles with paternal pride and tenderness. The other five sons – all older than the two boys – press around* DUCCIO, *the eldest. They stare up at their brothers hanging from the cornice, filled with envy and contempt, jealousy and anger.)*

DUCCIO: Always showing off, those two!

> *(The white elephant. The two brothers' paint brushes give it the finishing touch.* ANDREA *and* NICOLA *admire their finished work. They exchange a look of pride and admiration.)*

NICOLA: Finished!

ANDREA: Let's go down.

NICOLA: Shall I jump?
> (*Like acrobats, they grab hold of two ropes and leap into space.*
> *They swing down and land in front of the central door.*)

BONANNO: A seat.
> (*A chair is brought up for* BONANNO. *He sits down as though on*
> *a throne. His five oldest sons stand behind him, as* ANDREA *and*
> NICOLA *arrive coiling their ropes and sit down on either side of*
> *him. All stare in silence at the façade, now completely restored.*)

I'm sure whoever made this stood here, afterwards, to look
at it. In this very spot. They were superb – it's a miracle.
> (*As an arcane melody plays, the camera moves in on the*
> *cathedral façade, whose marble and colours gleam brightly in*
> *the spring sunlight.*)

(*Voice over*) I toast thee, church of Michele – and I toast our
grandfathers' grandfathers who had it built a thousand
years ago, and who handed this profession down to us – for
the hands – and the imagination.

3. INT. BONANNO HOUSEHOLD. DAY

A raised glass in his hand, old BONANNO *continues his toast,*
standing at the head of the table in the middle of a long medieval
room, where he and his seven children have their home and
workshop. The old man has invited his oldest assistants to dinner;
they are sitting along one side of the table. Across from them are the
five oldest offspring. Facing their father, at the end of the table, are
the two youngest brothers, ANDREA *and* NICOLA.

BONANNO: . . . Naturally I also toast you, for giving the
cathedral back the splendour it once had. And allow me to
thank my seven sons who worked with you.
> (*Everyone at the table raises a glass and takes a sip. The father*
> *is about to sit down . . . but thinks of something else. Suddenly*
> *a diabolic light appears in his eyes, half mischievous, half*
> *mocking, somewhere between tender and domineering. He*
> *straightens up again. After a hesitation, he raises his glass in a*
> *last toast.*)

And I want to make a special toast to – those two rascals down
there . . . (*Nods in the direction of* ANDREA *and* NICOLA.) . . .
my youngest, the ones with the golden hands. Master's hands.

22

(*A silence has fallen over the table. The father addresses the others in a conciliatory tone.*)

Anyhow, you're all good. Don't be offended if I single out those two scamps.

(NICOLA, *who had been smiling, suddenly turns serious and proud.* ANDREA, *who was serious, smiles and looks down. Their gazes meet and they exchange a conspiratorial look. Two of the elder brothers glare at them furiously, as though they'd been slapped in the face. Two other older brothers exchange a smouldering look, like a threat. The eldest of them,* DUCCIO, *keeps his head down gloomily. Then he angrily leaps to his feet and addresses his father in a choking voice.*)

DUCCIO: Fine, Papa, but I believe you wanted us all together to tell us something – something more important!

(*All eyes turn uneasily to* DUCCIO. *After a second he takes his seat, no less angrily. The other four brothers instinctively press around him. Their father is still standing; suddenly he looks aged. He bends his head.*)

BONANNO: Easy, boy. A son should never hurry his own father. I had planned to speak later – after the meal.

(*He sits down. A tense, embarrassed silence follows. Biting his lip in remorse,* DUCCIO *gets up, picks up a tray covered with a cloth and sets it humbly before his father. The cloth is snatched away and a miniature cathedral made out of marzipan and candy appears, resembling San Michele.* DUCCIO's *hand holds the knife out to his father. Instead, the old man draws his hand away. The father shakes his head to* DUCCIO *in tired sadness.*)

No, now that you've begun, I have to finish. (*Gathers his courage. Turns to his guests and children.*) Well, then. This is a farewell dinner. The work we completed today will be our last. We've been swept up in the crisis along with the rest. The firm is up to its neck in debts, and I'm forced to close down. What happens to it – that my seven sons will decide. I'm retiring to the country, to the house where I was born. (*Everyone stares at the old man in amazement and dismay. As though unable to stand those eyes on him,* BONANNO *continues with some impatience.*)

Anyway, you already knew it, didn't you? You could feel

which way the wind was blowing.
(*One of the artisans, as old as* BONANNO, *shakes his head.
He's all torn up. He can't – he won't – believe his ears.*)
OLD ARTISTAN: No! Not me – I didn't know a goddamn thing!
It's a complete shock.
(*He feels betrayed, tossed out on the street. He turns imploringly
to those around him, as though asking for support, to inveigh
against a great injustice.*)
This isn't a celebration; for me it's a funeral!
(*Without realizing it, he begins to shake so uncontrollably the
glass breaks in his hands. The sound of shattering glass sends a
shiver down* BONANNO'*s spine. He gives his old crony a look of
heart-breaking, impotent pity. All at once, the pain he had been
holding back explodes with unexpected violence.* BONANNO
*raises his fist and brings it down hard on the marzipan
cathedral. It smashes into a thousand flying pieces, while*
BONANNO *thunders in a terrible voice.*)
BONANNO: And for me? For me? What about for me?
(*The* OLD ARTISAN *stares at him. He stares at the
cake-splattered table. Getting hold of himself, he leaves the
table. He picks up his hat and silently slips out of the house.
Old* BONANNO *leans his head on his hand.*)
Forgive me.
(*He hides his face. Their faces streaming with tears,* ANDREA
and NICOLA *stand up silently and raise their glasses towards
their father and teacher. Everyone gets up and, imitating the
two brothers, lifts a glass to old* BONANNO.)
ONE OF THE COMPANY: To our master.

4. EXT. ROAD. DAY
In the street, the group of friends and co-workers leave the house.
DUCCIO *and the other older brothers are with them. They talk in low
voices.*
OLD WORKMAN: That's what you brothers have decided? To
sell everything?
DUCCIO: Everything. The buyer is going to make an emporium
out of the firm.
ANOTHER WORKMAN: What about you boys?

24

DUCCIO: They'll hire us all. It's a way for us to earn a living. We're not kids any more.

OLD WORKMAN: But you have to change profession! All seven? Even the two little brothers with the golden hands?

DUCCIO: (*Harshly*) Yes, all seven.

5. INT. BONANNO HOUSEHOLD. DAY

The brothers who had remained by their father's side tiptoe out of the room where the old man is resting. They close the door softly behind them, making a sign as though to say, 'Father's asleep.' In the doorway, DUCCIO nods. He too is tired; everybody is tired, the day is over. No, it isn't over: DUCCIO and his brothers' gazes are drawn like magnets to a sight that makes them frown. NICOLA and ANDREA, the two youngest, the two favourites, are still sitting at the uncleared table. The 'little' ones motion the 'big' ones to approach, while they talk animatedly between themselves, consulting some pieces of paper on which they've scribbled down notes and made drawings. Finally they turn to their brothers. Triumph is written on their faces.

NICOLA: We've gone over the accounts.

DUCCIO: Quiet, you'll wake Babbo.

NICOLA: Don't be discouraged.

ANDREA: We two have been thinking about it a lot. It's good to sell.

NICOLA: The company will continue without workmen, just us seven.

DUCCIO: Let's finish clearing up!
    (*With great force he pulls the tablecloth off the table, scattering* NICOLA's *and* ANDREA's *papers.* ANDREA *and* NICOLA *act with surprise at* DUCCIO's *violence.*)

ANDREA: For one year . . . For one year we won't take any pay.

NICOLA: Piero, you'd better not get married right now.

ANDREA: And all of you with families. No more children.

NICOLA: Explain it to your wives . . . !

DUCCIO: Quiet!

NICOLA: Are you afraid Babbo will hear us?
    (NICOLA *and* ANDREA *suddenly sense the wall of silence around them. They look up at their brothers' faces questioningly. The older brothers have formed a group at the other end of the table.*

26

They stare at NICOLA *and* ANDREA; *their eyes gleam with
hatred. The 'Little Brothers' are puzzled at first and try to
understand the situation.* NICOLA *thinks he sees what's wrong.*)
OK, Duccio. You explain. They're worried because Babbo
retired today, but us two . . . No . . . there'll be us
two . . . Du–

ANDREA: Duccio!
(*With a cry of rage, hatred and liberation, all five brothers leap
across the table and attack* ANDREA *and* NICOLA. *They separate*
ANDREA *and* NICOLA, *and then beat them up – one here, one
there.* ANDREA *and* NICOLA *disappear in a hail of punches.*)
(*In an unexpectedly infantile cry*) What are you doing?
(*His cry slows down the hail of punches. One by one, the
brothers let go of them.* ANDREA *and* NICOLA *seize their chance
to run to each other's arms.* ANDREA *repeats his childish wail.*)
What are you doing?
(NICOLA *chimes in.*)

NICOLA: Brothers!
(*His astonished, sorrowful 'Brothers!' sets the fire blazing
again. With one will, the brothers go back to beating* ANDREA
and NICOLA. *Dissolve to* –

6. EXT./INT. FATHER'S FARMHOUSE/COUNTRYSIDE. SUNSET
*The Tuscan countryside is touched by the last rays of the setting sun.
As night falls, the first fireflies appear glowing over the fields. The
camera pans to a secluded farmhouse belonging to old Bonanno.
Through the open door of Bonanno's house, the old man can be
glimpsed sitting in the middle of the room. On either side stand*
ANDREA *and* NICOLA.

ANDREA: (*Voice over*) Nicola and I went to see our father in his
house in the country . . . to say goodbye.
(*The father between his two sons. No lamp lights the room and
their three faces melt into the darkness. They speak quietly.*)

NICOLA: We won't come home till we have enough money to
buy back our company.

ANDREA: We'll work together again on our cathedrals, Papa. I
swear it.

NICOLA: Me too.

ANDREA: (*In a whisper*) But you wait for us, Papa.

NICOLA: Don't die!

> (*He bites his lip for having let it slip out. Their father's face can now be distinguished in the darkness. It is lined with tears. Silent tears, which he tries to hide behind a jovial smile.*)

BONANNO: I won't die. They say if you want to stay young, you have to act young. I'll behave like a kid. I swear it.

> (*Silence falls over them in the naked room: half choked with emotion, half embarrassed. A distant bell strikes eight.*)

> What time is it in America now?

ANDREA *and* NICOLA: (*With childish enthusiasm*) Morning!

BONANNO: Then when I fall asleep I'll say, 'Good morning, Andrea; good morning, Nicola.' The next evening I'll say, 'Good morning, Nicola; good morning, Andrea.' Because I'll never prefer one over the other. (*Lowers his voice still more, bending over his sons.*) There are two of you: that's your strength. As long as you remain equal. Otherwise you'll become enemies. Remember that: always equal in everything. That's your secret. A secret in two is a secret in God.

> (ANDREA's *voice drops, too, and almost quivers.*)

ANDREA: Papa, we're a little scared.

> (ANDREA *and* NICOLA *kneel at their father's side. The father crosses his hands on his chest, then raises them over his head, looking at his sons, in a strange, archaic blessing. Dissolve to:* ANDREA *and* NICOLA *hurrying down the road winding across the fields, where night has fallen and fireflies abound. They don't turn around to see . . . Their father standing in the middle of the yard. He stares out after his sons. He seems alone in the dark.*)

7. EXT. SHIP. DAY

A towering black wave: like a mountain of water, it seems to touch the wet sky. The smokestack of the ship sways. The furnaces have been fuelled to the maximum and give off a column of thick black smoke that immediately sinks in the air. On one wet, sooty side of the ship, someone has written: ADDIO ITALIA (*Farewell, Italy*). *A whitish glow from a lamp lights it. The camera pans lower with a fast dip to show another piece of graffito:* PORCA ITALIA (*Damn Italy*).

8. INT./EXT. SHIP. DAY

On a wobbly third-class table, two big bottles of wine clink against each other and break. The wine runs over the table in a red wave. The iron floor. One after another, plates of food fall and break on it, making a mess everywhere. One loaded plate slides across the table as the ship rolls. A spoon comes out of nowhere and scoops up some food, bringing it to an open mouth. The table tilts the other way and the plate slides again. Another spoon appears and takes a mouthful away. ANDREA *stubbornly eats his spoonful. Another movement of the ship slides the plate back down the table.* NICOLA *takes a bite in turn, obstinately ignoring the confusion around him. A black wave dashes against the side of the ship, wiping out* ADDIO ITALIA *and* PORCA ITALIA. *Dissolve to –*

9. INT. SHIP. EVENING

The roar has been replaced by silence. It is evening. A pile of beat-up hemp suitcases, packages and rags have been shoved up against the walls of a big third-class room. A quiet voice breaks the silence.

IMMIGRANT: (*Out of shot*) They say we're here – in America.

ANOTHER VOICE: (*Out of shot*) Who said so?

> (*The camera rises to reveal the porthole, filthy from water and smoke. Through it, the shapes of tall buildings can be glimpsed. The lights in the windows shine in the darkness.* NICOLA *and* ANDREA *stare at it in fascination, all choked up. Their faces slowly dissolve into the faces of two little boys with the same expression, as they gaze at . . . A big Christmas tree in the kitchen of their old home. The tree gleams with light. The boys' eyes light up, too, at the sight of these magic lights. The image dissolves to . . . The faces of* NICOLA *and* ANDREA *on the ship, looking up at the skyscraper.*)

ANDREA: Hello, America!

NICOLA: Damn America, you'll be ours!

> (*Dissolve to –*)

10. EXT. WESTERN LANDSCAPE. DAY

Blackbirds are seen in the light blue sky.

ANDREA: (*Voice over*) Instead, America did not become ours.

NICOLA: (*Voice over*) Time passed. We moved from state to

state, while our jobs kept getting more temporary and humiliating.

(*A harsh range just this side of a desert, somewhere in the West. Dusty hills covered with scrub brush stretch out as far as the eye can see. Running around in the middle of a herd of grunting, squealing pigs,* ANDREA *and* NICOLA *shout at them and try to get them into their pens. The brothers are unrecognizable. Their faces are hollowed out, their beards straggly and unkempt, their eyes red, and a harsh, almost mean curl has appeared on their lips.* NICOLA *shouts at his brother in Italian.*)

NICOLA: I'm missing six pigs. Are they with yours, Andrea?

(*After a second's silence,* ANDREA *shouts back in English.*)

ANDREA: Ask me in English or I won't answer!

(NICOLA *shoots his brother a look of exasperation.* ANDREA *doesn't say a word.* NICOLA *closes the gate of the pen and starts off for the valley, shouting in Italian again.*)

NICOLA: I'm going back to look for them.

(ANDREA *bites his lip glumly.* NICOLA's *tiny, lost figure*

descends into the rocky valley leading up to a hill. He turns
around and sees ANDREA *at his heels, coming to help him.)*

ANDREA: (*Conciliatory, but still in English*) Wait! Where did you
see them last?

NICOLA: (*In laboured English*) On the rich . . .

ANDREA: (*Correcting his pronunciation*) Not 'rich', Nicola,
'ridge'.

(NICOLA *doesn't answer him. The two brothers push on further
and further into the valley, fanning out to cover more territory.
Suddenly* NICOLA *lets out a yell, venting his frustration.*)

NICOLA: It is useless, Andrea! It was all useless!

(*His voice echoes shrilly and unnaturally in the great silence,
doubling back in a distant echo. Even* ANDREA *starts shouting
in Italian now, with strength born of desperation.*)

ANDREA: No! If we talked better, we would not be here now!

(NICOLA *looks around him: a soulless desert. There is an almost
childish note of fear in his question.*)

NICOLA: Will we be here always, Andrea?

(ANDREA *doesn't answer. He doesn't know what to say. An
echo repeats* NICOLA's *anxious question. As though to exorcize
it,* ANDREA *raises his voice again, harshly.*)

ANDREA: No! Nicola, repeat after me: 'One, two, buckle the
shoe! . . . One, two, buckle the shoe!'

(NICOLA *responds, but the farther the two brothers wander into
the mountains, the more his answers sound like angry sobs,
laments of protest.*)

NICOLA: 'One, two, buckle the shoe!'

ANDREA *and* NICOLA: 'Three, four, knock at the door! Five,
six, pick up sticks! Five, six, pick up sticks! Seven, eight,
lay them straight! Seven, eight, lay them straight! Nine,
ten, a big fat hen!'

ANDREA: To come.

NICOLA: Came. Come.

ANDREA: To buy.

NICOLA: Bought. Bought – Bought! Bought!

(*Several big birds appear wheeling around overhead: vultures.
On the other side of the mountain ridge, between the rocks, lie
the bodies of two dead pigs. Four other pigs are digging around*

32

them. They are trying to eat them. They tear them to pieces and drag the pieces away).

ANDREA: They fell off the cliff!

NICOLA: They eat each other!

ANDREA: Get the others away!

(ANDREA *and* NICOLA *fly down the mountainside. Kicking and hitting the pigs with their sticks, they try to shoo the stubborn cannibals away from their prey.* ANDREA *rains blow after blow on their heads. The struggle is grotesque and macabre. The pigs are rounded up at last.* ANDREA's *back rises and falls with nervous heaving. All at once a vulture plunges down on him; it claws his shoulder with a horrible squawking sound. Shivering with horror,* ANDREA *lets out a chilling scream. He writhes. He jumps to his feet. He spins around like a madman. He flaps his arms. A big stick comes down hard, knocking the vulture to the ground.* NICOLA *has wielded the blow. Now he stands in stupefaction, looking at . . . his brother huddled on the ground, shaken by trembling and disgust, as he keeps repeating in a hoarse voice –)*

Disgusting – disgusting – disgusting!

11. EXT. ROAD THROUGH THE DESERT. DAY
A wagon rumbles along a dusty road through the wilderness. The silence is so intense it is almost unbearable, like the light and the heat of the sun. His head hanging with weariness, NICOLA *is driving, while* ANDREA *lies down in the back.* ANDREA *seems to have fallen asleep; instead he is wide awake.*

12. INT. BONANNO'S FARMHOUSE BEDROOM. NIGHT
Old BONANNO *is preparing to retire. He stands beside his bed in the bare bedroom of the old farmhouse. A single lamp lights the room. He turns back the sheets and lays down on the bed. He blows out the lamp. The old man's face in the darkness. His eyes are wide open. He stares into the dark.*

BONANNO: Good morning, Nicola! Good morning, Andrea!

13. EXT. WESTERN LANDSCAPE. DAWN
As though in answer to the old man's greeting, dawn is rising over the

bleak western range. ANDREA *is fast asleep, leaning against the back of the wagon that lurches on down the road.* NICOLA, *in the driver's seat, has also fallen asleep. The horse's hooves pound the road. Then we see the road is a railway track. Long shot: the wagon with the two sleeping brothers aboard lurches down the middle of a railway track crossing a desert plain. The camera pans to show a train coming, still some distance away, from the opposite direction. The horse and wagon stumble on. The black locomotive speeding along. The wagon wheels rolling to the right. The train wheels rolling to the left. The wagon and the train are heading straight at each other. A few yards separate them when with an ear-splitting shriek of brakes, the train grinds to a halt. The train wheels send off sparks from the friction. The horse rears.* NICOLA *forces his eyes open. For a second, seeing the black hulk of the locomotive in front of him, he thinks he's dreaming. Then he shoots to his feet in terror, while* ANDREA *pops up behind him, his mouth and eyes gaping. The brothers jump down from the wagon. Two engineers leap down from the train. They shout at them. Passengers' faces appear in the windows, as they try to find out what happened. The* ENGINEER *driving the locomotive, who is*

*almost in shock, wants to beat them up, while the brothers try to
justify themselves in a confused mixture of English and Italian. The
engineer's assistant stops him from doing anything foolish and shouts
reassurance at the passengers.*

BRAKEMAN: What in tarnation's up there?

TRAINMAN: Team of horses.

ENGINEER: Good living God . . . What the hell do they think
they're doing?
(ANDREA *and* NICOLA *are moving the wagon off the tracks.
The* ENGINEER *and* BRAKEMAN *descend from the train.*)
Can you believe it?

BRAKEMAN: The brake's blocked, Jeff!

ENGINEER: Oh Christ! You damned fool sons o' bitches!

TRAINMAN: (*Trying to calm down the* ENGINEER) Easy, take it
easy!

ENGINEER: (*Approaching* ANDREA *and* NICOLA) I ought to tear
their heads off . . . 's what I ought to do!

NICOLA: One moment . . . One moment.

ENGINEER: Sound like foreigners to me.

TRAINMAN: It's OK, just take it easy, huh. No point in getting
. . . yeah . . . (*To the passengers who are getting off the train*)
It's OK, folks. We'll be off in no time. Now, just get back
and sit tight . . .

ENGINEER: Yeah, for an hour. Cinders reached the smoke-box.

TRAINMAN: Oh, great!

ENGINEER: The brake shoes are jammed, take some time for
them to cool off. No-good bastards!
(*The passengers start getting back on the train. The* TRAINMAN
pushes the ENGINEER *back on the locomotive.* ANDREA *and*
NICOLA *are adjusting the wagon when a distant voice comes
floating in the air. It is a fine baritone, who begins singing the
verses of a heartrending, tender song in Italian. The voice is
then joined by a chorus of male voices, Italian voices, intoning
the great prayer from Verdi's* La Forza del Destino.)

MALE CHORUS: . . . la vergine degli angeli . . . ci copra del suo
manto . . .
(NICOLA *turns in amazement, trying to see where it's coming
from, and meets* . . . ANDREA's *equally stupefied face, his head*

35

cocked toward . . . The train on the tracks. The Italian chorus
seems to be coming from the last carriage. ANDREA *and*
NICOLA *instinctively draw close to one another, looking.*
Travelling shot down the length of the train to the last carriage,
from which the Verdi chorus is growing in power and intensity.)
. . . e ci pròtegga l'angelo santo . . .
(The first verse ends. There is a second of silence. Then two
solitary voices answer with the second verse. They belong to
ANDREA *and* NICOLA, *who warble uncertainly. The camera*
gently pans to reveal the two brothers standing motionless beside
the wagon, singing. After a moment of amazement, the chorus
in the train starts up again, joining in with the two solitary
voices at a higher register. Dissolve to . . . Some of the Italians
have got off the train and are talking to ANDREA *and* NICOLA.
The others are all peering out of the window with friendly
cordiality. Their chorus leaders, who are also the foremen,
explain with a grin.)

FIRST FOREMAN: No, we aren't the chorus of the Opera – just a
touch of nostalgia. We're all artisans: sculptors, plasterers,
marble carvers . . .

YOUNG MAN AT WINDOW: Carpenters!

FIRST FOREMAN: That kind of thing . . .

VOICE: And painters!

SECOND FOREMAN: We're off to the San Francisco Expo.
We're building the Italian Pavilion. He and I are the two
foremen.

FIRST FOREMAN: Those guys are fresh out of Italy. The others
were already here. How about you two?

ANDREA: (*With great dignity*) Artisans like you.

NICOLA: Tuscans.

ANDREA: I don't know if you know it, but we restored the
Cathedral of the Miracles.

FIRST FOREMAN: So what are you doing here?
(*The man suddenly falls silent in front of . . . the abruptly*
innocent, desperate faces of the two young men. They seem like
two kids again. The ENGINEER *blows his horn. The train*
slowly starts chugging forward. The train is gathering speed.
The last carriage goes by, too, revealing ANDREA *and* NICOLA

alone again, standing motionless by the side of the tracks. The plain behind them is empty and desolate. ANDREA *and* NICOLA *watch the train chugging away. They turn to each other, and in their eyes a look of mysterious agreement appears. Their mutual decision has all the violence of the music that now resounds with the strength of a full orchestra, playing Verdi's Great Prayer.* ANDREA *and* NICOLA *slowly look up at the train. The brothers begin a mad dash behind it, urged on by the music. On the back of the last carriage, the* FIRST FOREMAN *and the other Italians see what they're trying to do and shout encouragement, holding out their arms.* NICOLA *and* ANDREA *reach the carriage with a last great effort, grab hold of the railing, helping each other. At last they leap aboard, welcomed by the applause of the Italians. Panting happily, bent double from the effort,* ANDREA *raises his head. And up in the sky he sees something he points out to his brother. Overhead a vulture circles.* NICOLA *is looking at it too, now. His arm makes a triumphal, obscene gesture at the bird, while the orchestra concludes the Great Prayer with a last, sublime chord. The train races over the great plain on its way to San Francisco. Fade out.)*

14. EXPOSITION MONTAGE
A rapid montage showing the San Francisco Exposition. The sequence begins with the lights from a projector. There then follows a series of images from the Exposition, culminating in a sequence about the diamond tower built by the Italians. This sequence contains a newspaper photograph of the construction team of the Diamond Tower. In the middle are the two FOREMEN; *grouped around them are the others. The camera zooms in on two faces:* ANDREA *and* NICOLA.

NICOLA: (*Voice over*) We did ourselves proud. All the Italians did themselves proud that year in San Francisco. We were the heroes of the hour. Nobody talked about anything but us and our Tower of Jewels . . . We worked there as day labourers. We made some money . . . Bought ourselves some fancy new suits.

ANDREA: (*Voice over*) At the Expo they were showing the moving picture of *Cabiria*, another great Italian success!

15. EXT. SAN FRANCISCO MOVIE THEATRE. NIGHT

The entrance to a big San Francisco theatre. A huge crowd of people is standing in line to get in. The lights on the marquee flash: CABIRIA. *The crowd is pushing to get into the theatre: the camera seems to single out one film-goer in particular.*

ANDREA: (*Voice over*) There was one man in the crowd who wanted to see the picture again, at once, by himself. He paid for the theatre and orchestra.

16. INT. SAN FRANCISCO MOVIE THEATRE. NIGHT

The film has just finished. The orchestra is leaving. Seen from behind, D. W. GRIFFITH *is sitting alone on a seat in the middle of the theatre. He is wearing a wide-brimmed hat.*

ANDREA: (*Voice over*) That man, destined to have a great influence over our lives, was the most famous film director in all of America, D. W. Griffith.

(*The words* THE END *appear on the screen. The members of the orchestra hurriedly put their instruments away and trickle out. From the projection room come two beams that light up parts of the seats. In backlighting:* GRIFFITH *remains seated. He is lost in thought. Then he murmurs to someone sitting in front of him.*)

GRIFFITH: Send a wire: To Pastrone, director of *Cabiria*, Italy. 'Your picture is greater than all of mine.'

(*From behind, a woman's hand rests gently on his shoulder. It is his wife.* GRIFFITH *starts dictating again.*)

'Tonight, you made me realize the film I'm shooting is taking me off course. I am cancelling it.'

(GRIFFITH'*s closest assistants, who are scattered here and there throughout the theatre, jump to their feet in surprise and dismay.*)

THOMPSON: He said, 'Cancel', Mr Grass. Did I hear correctly?

GRASS: But we've . . . we've already made the calls for Monday . . . Tom?

TOM: That's right: a hundred extras; six automobiles.

MICHAEL: Should we call the actors?

THOMPSON: Wait a minute, just shut up!

GRASS: Mr Griffith, we have . . .

(*The assistants start moving towards* GRIFFITH, *who stands up from his seat.*)

GRIFFITH: Enough! Add: 'I don't know whether to be grateful or to hate you. D. W. Griffith.' (*Goes to the* ASSISTANT, *takes the telegram and tears it up.*) Never mind. Artists communicate through their work.

17. EXT./INT. SAN FRANCISCO MOVIE THEATRE/CAR. NIGHT
Reporters crowd around GRIFFITH.

FIRST REPORTER: There he is!

SECOND REPORTER: Mr Griffith, sir! Have the Italians done it again?

FIRST REPORTER: How does it compare?

SECOND REPORTER: What impressed you most about *Cabiria*?

GRIFFITH: Everything!

THIRD REPORTER: A sequence or an image . . . ?

GRIFFITH: The elephant.

THIRD REPORTER: What?

GRIFFITH: The black elephant! Thompson, would you bring Mrs Griffith?

THOMPSON: Yes, sir.

SECOND REPORTER: Is it true you plan to stop production of your present film?

GRIFFITH: It is.

THIRD REPORTER: A disaster!

(GRIFFITH *moves towards his car.*)

GRIFFITH: A stroke of luck.

THIRD REPORTER: How's that, sir?

GRIFFITH: I shall transform it! It will become part of a fresco.

SECOND REPORTER: Then you'll resume production?

THIRD REPORTER: Along the lines of the Italians' *Cabiria*, sir?

GRIFFITH: Three hundred times greater than *Cabiria*!

(*The car zooms off. Inside the moving car. Rain beats at the window-panes.* GRIFFITH *has collapsed against the back of the seat, thinking hard. He has taken his hat off. In the darkness his wife is close to him.*)

MRS GRIFFITH: (*Quietly*) Are you thinking about your old idea?

(GRIFFITH *looks at his wife gratefully. He nods.*)

Intolerance. I can always tell when it crops up in your head. (GRIFFITH *lets his head fall back again in the obscurity of the car, and slowly a mysterious smile comes over his face. Music rises on the soundtrack. Mysterious, too, are the strange lights that reflect off the windows, which gleam with raindrops. The music grows more sweeping.* GRIFFITH *seems almost entranced by the lights . . . the lights coming off the Diamond Tower.* GRIFFITH *rolls down his window from the point of view of the moving car: in the distance, the Diamond Tower gleams in the night in the torrential rain.*)

GRIFFITH: Go closer.

18. EXT. FAIRGROUNDS. NIGHT

The car has come to a stop in the pouring rain. GRIFFITH *steps out. His wife urges him to take shelter under something.*

MRS GRIFFITH: David, what are you doing? It's pouring!

    (GRIFFITH *is once more impatient and aggressive.*)

GRIFFITH: Who built this?

    (*The tower seen from below: awe-inspiring, marvellous in its plaster work and bas-reliefs. The other two cars of his retinue have stopped. Griffith's assistants follow him out into the rain.*)

THOMPSON: The Italians. It's the Italian pavilion, Mr Griffith.

GRASS: Italians, Mr Griffith! It's always the Italians!

GRIFFITH: Those darn Italians! I want them.

THOMPSON: They must be gone by now, Mr Griffith.

GRASS: They finished building the Expo a month ago.

GRIFFITH: Find them. I want the men who built this thing. They have to go to work for me! I want the construction foreman, Mr Grass.

    (GRIFFITH *takes his hat off, and places it on his wife's head.*)

MRS GRIFFITH: *Intolerance!*

19. INT. ITALIAN CIRCLE OF SAN FRANCISCO. DAY

A big room. Behind a counter an EMPLOYEE *answers the telephone. We catch the conversation in the middle.*

EMPLOYEE: The two artisans you want are leaving for Italy today with most of their workers. I know because they are members of this Italian Club. The two foremen who

worked on the Expo. Look, if you leave your number, I will try to get in touch . . .
(*A fast pan unexpectedly reveals* ANDREA *and* NICOLA, *tensely awaiting the outcome of the call.*)
You are calling from where? Hollywood? To make elephants? Oh! Griffith? One moment, hold on. (*Turns towards* ANDREA *and* NICOLA.) No good. They've got as many workmen as they need. They just want the two foremen . . . (*Goes back to his conversation with Hollywood.*) All right, if I happen to find anything, who should I call? Ah, send them to Frisco . . . And then?
(*As the* EMPLOYEE *continues speaking,* ANDREA *and* NICOLA *look at each other.*)
ANDREA: They want Teddoro and Amilcare.
EMPLOYEE: And a truck will pick them up, OK. Goodbye.
(*Looks at* ANDREA *and* NICOLA.) They want . . .
NICOLA: We can find them . . .
ANDREA: They sail for Seattle in one hour.
EMPLOYEE: Yes.
NICOLA: Maybe we can stop them.

20. EXT. STREETS OF SAN FRANCISCO. DAY
The tiny figures of ANDREA *and* NICOLA *running like mad. They race along the rough wall of the port. Suddenly* ANDREA *slows down. He stops. The music stops with him. He bends down to tie his shoe.*
NICOLA, *who has gone on running, turns around, goes back and gives his brother a quizzical look.*
NICOLA: We'll be too late!
(ANDREA *slowly raises his eyes and, in the silent void left by the music, pronounces his words deliberately.*)
ANDREA: Better! If they left, then we can try ourselves. (*As though to justify himself, he adds an excuse.*) My shoe came untied.
(NICOLA *catches his drift. He looks down at his own shoes.*)
NICOLA: Both of mine are.
(NICOLA's *shoes are perfectly tied. His hands comes into frame and unties them.* NICOLA *straightens up. He starts walking again with his laces untied, slowly, with exaggerated difficulty.* ANDREA *follows on his heels.*)

42

21. EXT. PORT WHARF. DAY
The wharf is deserted; the boat has already left. NICOLA's *and* ANDREA's *feet run up and stop on the edge of the parapet.* NICOLA's *shoes are still untied. Pan over the brothers as they stare out over the quay.*

NICOLA: God, I'm sorry! (*Pauses, thinking. Then his eyes sparkle.*) But I'm glad, too!

22. EXT. TRUCK GARAGE. DAY
NICOLA *and* ANDREA *are standing behind the truck. A* DISPATCHER *is questioning them and taking notes in a little book.*

DISPATCHER: So, you guys are uh . . . ?
    (NICOLA *forces the words out of his throat.*)

NICOLA: The foremen your director wants.

ANDREA: The director's name is Griffith, right?
    (*The* DISPATCHER *nods.*)

DISPATCHER: Hang on a minute. OK, we're set.
    (*The brothers leap into the back of the truck, but are stopped again by the* DISPATCHER's *voice.*)
    Your names?
    (*They hesitate uncertainly for a second. Then, resolutely, they lie.*)

ANDREA: Amilcare Martini.

NICOLA: Teodoro Benvenuti.
    (*The* DISPATCHER *takes note.*)

DISPATCHER: OK, hop in, *paesans!* The day after tomorrow, you'll be in Hollywood . . . !
    (*The two back doors of the truck swing shut, showing the legend* TRIANGLE CORPORATION, *Griffith's film company. Below it, in big red letters, is written:* HOLLYWOOD.)
    (*To the* DRIVER) All yours . . . Don't forget to fill up at Salinas', OK!
    (*The truck takes off.*)

23. EXT. CALIFORNIA ROADS. DAY/NIGHT
The truck races across vast stretches of California desert.

24. EXT. HOLLYWOOD HILLS. MORNING
It's so foggy you can hardly make out the road sign announcing

HOLLYWOOD. *The truck drops off the two brothers, who leap into thick fog. The* DRIVER *leans out of the window.*

DRIVER: I'll leave you here. The trolley will take you straight to Mr Grass's office. He's the production manager for Mr Griffith. See you around!

ANDREA: Thank you!

(*The truck drives off. The brothers can't see a thing or get their bearings. All is fog and silence; a valley of the dead. They sit under the road sign. A shiver runs down their spines when, through the fog, a distant voice calls out to them. It is the voice of an old man hoarsely shouting.*)

OLD MAN: (*Voice over*) My sons!

(*As though guided by the brothers' eyes, the camera pans to scrutinize the fog. The voice comes again.*)

Go, my sons! Yes, my sons. I await you.

(NICOLA *and* ANDREA *have a suspicion they've really gone mad. They laugh, but the sound of their laughter scares them even more.* ANDREA *turns serious.*)

ANDREA: Where are we?

(*The fog begins to disappear, revealing a hill. A group of medieval knights in white robes is scattered across the hill, which is crowned with an enormous oak. The camera pans away from the knights revealing first, a film crew getting ready to shoot, and then, hidden behind the trees, a small orchestra which begins to play on the word 'Action'.*)

DIRECTOR: All right, roll 'em! Action!

(*Two young knights, riding on white horses appear. They ride down towards the oak where the* KING *is sitting. The horsemen reach the* KING *their father and kneel on either side of him. The* KING *puts his hands on their heads.*)

OLD KING: Go my sons! I shall wait for you. We have been defeated, but when you return, you'll win back my kingdom!

(*The two sons stand up. At the same moment* NICOLA *stands up from where he and* ANDREA *have been sitting.*)

NICOLA: Look, Andrea – the old king is crying.

(*The old* KING. *In spite of his proud demeanour, two tears are trickling down his wrinkled cheeks. Enthralled by the sight, the*

44

*two brothers don't realize that the red Hollywood trolley has
silently come up behind them. To keep from running them down,
the* CONDUCTOR *suddenly honks his horn and brings them back
to reality.)*

25. INT. TROLLEY. DAY
*The car is moving. It is crowded with people on their way to work.
Most of them are young, lively, friendly; they know each other.
Some are already in costume. A famous* ACTOR *has got on with his
whole family, and his wife is handing out sandwiches from a picnic
basket.*

LADY: *(Seeing* ANDREA *and* NICOLA*)* Are you kids new?
  *(*ANDREA *starts to say 'no', to look good, but disarmed by the
  woman's cordiality he nods.)*
  (Giving ANDREA *a sandwich)* Have a piece.
ANDREA: Thank you.
  *(*ANDREA *splits the sandwich with* NICOLA. *Two girls
  are sitting nearby.* EDNA *is more serious than her friend*
  MABEL, *who is protesting for both of them to the production
  assistant,* THOMPSON, *who looks sorry he can't help
  them.)*
MABEL: Just give us a chance – we're dancers.
  (A Venetian woman sitting nearby:)
MARGA: Yes, and very good ones.
  *(*NICOLA *and* ANDREA *stare at the girls intently.)*
EDNA: We can't be extras all our lives!
THOMPSON: Look, girls, it's not up to me . . .
EDNA: But even you don't believe us, do you?
THOMPSON: Well, can you do a split?
EDNA: Sure!
  *(*EDNA *stands up and, while the other passengers look on in
  amusement, does a perfect split.* MABEL *imitates her, ending in
  an even more spectacular split. Everybody claps. The two girls
  return to their seats, in triumph.* NICOLA *and* ANDREA *also
  clap their hands and laugh. The red streetcar clatters merrily on,
  but, suddenly, there's an obstacle on the tracks: a big mobile
  crane with several men working around a camera mounted on
  top. The trolley has to slam on its brakes.*

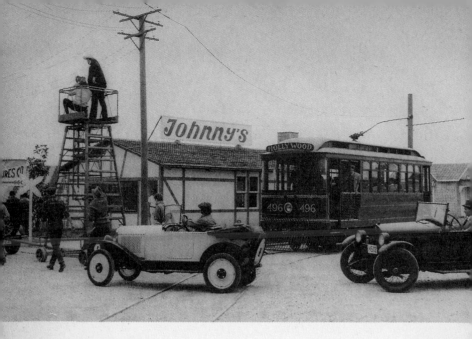

26. EXT. STREET. DAY

WORKERS: (*At the base of the crane*) Let Mr Griffith get up
there! . . . What do you need, sir?

27. INT. TROLLEY. DAY

THOMPSON: It's Griffith, trying out his new machine.
(*At the name of Griffith,* ANDREA's *and* NICOLA's *ears prick
up.* NICOLA *and* ANDREA *rush to the front of the car.*)
ANDREA: Griffith? It's Griffith!
NICOLA: It's Griffith! Where's Griffith?
ANDREA: Which one is he?
THOMPSON: He's the man on the crane with the big white hat.
Good morning, Mr Griffith!

28. EXT. STREET. DAY

GRIFFITH: Good morning to you, Mr Thompson. (*To the
workers at the bottom of the crane*) Let's go!
(ANDREA *and* NICOLA *start shouting.*)
ANDREA and NICOLA: Mr Griffith!

46

(D. W. GRIFFITH *turns around, trying to see who's calling him.* ANDREA *and* NICOLA *lean out of the window of the trolley, which is moving again. They go on shouting.*)

ANDREA and NICOLA: Mr Griffith! We are the Italians!

(GRIFFITH *responds to this strange greeting with a hesitant, questioning smile, while the crane truck drives off with him in the opposite direction.*)

29. EXT. HOLLYWOOD STUDIO. DAY

THOMPSON *is supervising the destruction of a model of an elephant.*

THOMPSON: Pull her down! Destroy her! Mr Griffith says he doesn't even want the tail left!

30. INT. HOLLYWOOD STUDIO. DAY

GRASS, *who is in charge of production, is sitting behind his desk. Behind him is a huge board with drawings of elephants tacked on it.*

GRASS: (*Ironically*) So you two are the famous Italian builders?

(ANDREA *and* NICOLA *are standing in front of him.*)

ANDREA and NICOLA: (*In unison*) Yes.

GRASS: You're here to make the elephants for *Intolerance*.

ANDREA *and* NICOLA: Yes.

GRASS: (*Pointing to the drawings behind him*) None of our drawings has met with the approval of Mr Griffith, but you Italians think you're going to do better. Great.

(THOMPSON, *a young man of irrepressible enthusiasm, comes up with a newspaper in his hand; there is an article in it about the San Francisco Expo. He shows it to* GRASS.)

THOMPSON: Remember what they did up in Frisco!

(*He lays it on the table. A photo of the Diamond Tower. Pan to a picture of the Italian team. In the centre, very clearly, stand the two* FOREMEN. *Around them are the others, including* ANDREA *and* NICOLA. GRASS *gives the paper a bored glance and pushes it away.*)

GRASS: I know, I know . . .

(*He looks thoughtful. He picks up the paper again and stares at it intently.* ANDREA *and* NICOLA *are frozen to the spot, waiting for the catastrophe.* GRASS *stares at the group picture, looks up at the brothers, and looks back at the picture. The two*

brothers in the photo.)

I see Hollywood agrees with you, my dear architects. You look thirty years younger!

(ANDREA *and* NICOLA *gulp. They're crushed.* ANDREA *struggles to find his voice.*)

ANDREA: We just thought we . . . Can we sit down?

(*Without waiting for an answer, he drops into a chair.* NICOLA *collapses beside him. An uncomfortable silence has fallen over the office.* GRASS *begins speaking in measured tones.*)

GRASS: Have you been in the service?

(*They hastily answer in unison.*)

ANDREA and NICOLA: Yes.

GRASS: Then on your feet. About face. Forward – March! Hup–two, hup–two, hup . . .

(*The brothers stand as though hypnotized.*)

(*Louder*) Hup–two, hup–two, hup–two, hup–two . . . !

(*The two brothers immediately respond and march out of the room.*)

31. EXT. STAGE SET. DAY

Outside the door, confused and humiliated, ANDREA *and* NICOLA *look around them without knowing which way to go. Chaos reigns everywhere. Not far away, several groups of extras take their places on the set of a comic short. It is a restaurant scene. There are no projectors, and natural sunlight is being used.*

UNIT DIRECTOR: Actors and extras, on stage! Take your positions! No! You, no. Come on, come on! Hurry it up, please!

(*The* UNIT DIRECTOR *has turned to the two girls,* MABEL *and* EDNA. *They are extras today.*)

You too, girls. Aren't you extras? . . . Get a move on there!

(*The girls reluctantly obey.*)

MABEL: Extras, extras . . .

EDNA: Extras . . .

(GRASS *steps out of his office and quickly strides towards the set.* THOMPSON *trots behind him. When he sees* ANDREA *and* NICOLA, *he runs back to them.*)

THOMPSON: Sorry I got you in trouble. I always have to go and open my big mouth!

(GRASS *shouts to the* DIRECTOR *of the comedy.*)

GRASS: Steve, finish up here by tonight! Tomorrow I'm pulling it. I got to get the sets for Griffith ready. (*Turns around and finds the two brothers standing behind him.*) You still here?

(NICOLA *and* ANDREA *answer with humble dignity.*)

ANDREA: We were wrong, Mr Grass. We have to pay.

NICOLA: We need a job – any kind of job.

(GRASS *is too furious to even listen to them.*)

GRASS: Yeah, sure. No, no! I know you wops! Liars, wheedlers, allergic to work, belly in the sun and hands on your belly!

(NICOLA *glances at* ANDREA, *bites his tongue as hard as he can and twists his hands. He can't resist. Suddenly leaping forward, he grabs his brother's hands, lifts them in the air and shows them to* GRASS, *shouting.*)

NICOLA: These hands have restored the cathedrals of Pisa, Lucca and Florence!

ANDREA: Whose sons are you? We are the sons of the sons of the sons of Michelangelo and Leonardo!

(*He would carry on and say even more, but he gets hold of himself and stops. Silence has fallen around them.* NICOLA *lowers his voice.*)

NICOLA: No, excuse us. We are only here to ask for jobs.

(*From the mass of extras, a female voice pipes up.*)

MABEL: Viva Firenze!

(*It is* MABEL. EDNA *is standing beside her.*)

EDNA: Viva Firenze! We were in Florence once!

MABEL: It's the most beautiful place in the world!

ANDREA: Viva Firenze!

(*An icy silence falls again.* GRASS *doesn't know what to say. He looks to the left and right, and finally shouts.*)

GRASS: The sun's going!

STEVE: Will you take your places . . . ! Music!

(*A comic chase ensues around the restaurant tables, climaxing with the inescapable pies in the face.* NICOLA *and* ANDREA *have been touched by the girls' sympathy for their plight, and try to spot them in the middle of all that confusion. They see them. In spite of being caught up in the fast-moving comedy,* MABEL

and EDNA *return their glances. They stop, smiling.* MABEL
suddenly ducks to keep from being hit by a pie, which gets
EDNA *square in the face instead.* MABEL *straightens up and*
can't hold back a laugh. But a second pie gets her, too. The
brothers don't know whether to laugh or be concerned about the
girls.)

32. EXT. END OF THE TROLLEY LINE. NIGHT

The tramline ends in a field on the outskirts of Hollywood. It's night:
a starry night, with fireflies glowing all around. In the moonlight, the
big red sail of a Viking ship sitting on the grass waves mysteriously.
The trolley swings around on a turning platform until it faces the
opposite direction. The place is practically deserted. NICOLA *and*
ANDREA *stand on the ground with their suitcases in hand and ask*
the CONDUCTOR *a question while he turns around.*

NICOLA: Do you go by the train station?

CONDUCTOR: No, no, next car. After midnight.

> (*As it turns, the trolley reveals* MABEL *and* EDNA *sitting in the*
> *back, tired and self-absorbed. They're even prettier in the*
> *evening light. The brothers see them. The two girls see them,*
> *too.*)

EDNA: Hey, it's those two boys again.

MABEL: What? . . . It's them!

> (NICOLA *and* ANDREA *look as if they might go over to talk to*
> *them, but then think the better of it, exchange a few words in a*
> *low voice, smile at them again, and walk away. The girls look*
> *surprised and a little disappointed.*)

EDNA and MABEL: Hm!

> (NICOLA *and* ANDREA *walk though the dark field, shadows in*
> *the darkness, and catch fireflies. The girls turn their backs to the*
> *windows. Two fists knock on the glass and make them turn*
> *around again. They lean out. The four young people stare at*
> *each other: the women in amazement, the men with tenderness.*
> *The fireflies pass from the men's hands to the women's. But the*
> *streetcar is ringing its bell. It starts moving. The four hardly*
> *have time to say goodbye. The boys watch the trolley grow*
> *distant and disappear into the darkness.*)

33. EXT. END OF TROLLEY LINE/ROTUNDA. NIGHT

NICOLA *and* ANDREA *are still sitting, half asleep on the rotunda, which is pulsating with fireflies. All at once the headlights of a broken-down jalopy hit them.* THOMPSON *leans out of the car.*

THOMPSON: Can you guys take care of birds?

ANDREA and NICOLA: Birds? Yes!

THOMPSON: Then I got a job for you. Hop in!

> (*They get in. The car drives through the dark towards a wooded hill.*)

We got a hundred birds for a scene we're gonna shoot in a couple of weeks. Just feed 'em and clean the cages morning and night. During the day I'll try to find you odd jobs on the set. At night you can sleep in the birdhouse.

> (*His headlights pick up a rambling, secluded old building. It stands between the woods and a clearing.*)

Well, this is it. You can get out. The door's open.

> (*Seeing the brothers' uncertain expression, he laughs.*)

What's the matter? You scared?

> (*The brothers scramble out. And with that he drives off.* NICOLA *and* ANDREA *are left standing there in the dark. Then, almost automatically, they walk to the door.* ANDREA *slips the key in and jumps.*)

ANDREA: We didn't even tell him thanks!

34. INT. BIRDHOUSE. NIGHT

The brothers step inside. They are immediately hit by an infernal shrieking: the whole place is full of cages. Birds of every description, awakened by the boys' flashlight, start screaming their heads off.

NICOLA: What a stink!

> (*On the floor are two dubious-looking straw mattresses. Without looking at them* NICOLA *and* ANDREA *collapse on to them. They lie on the straw mattresses, their eyes staring into the dark.*)

ANDREA: I'd die of pity if I saw somebody like you and me.

NICOLA: Good morning, Babbo.

> (*The camera moves in on the cages animated with strange birds, while the image dissolves into the cathedral of San Michele in Tuscany, glowing in the clear morning light. Fade out.*)

35. INT. STAGE SET. DAY

*A group of dancers wait in the dark for the beginning of a difficult shot.
In the darkness, the* CAMERAMAN, *the* DIRECTOR *and other members
of the crew wait for a signal.* NICOLA *is standing with two poles
waiting. He casts a quick glance at* ANDREA . . . ANDREA *is perched
on another level, checking a hole made in the studio wall and covered
with a piece of wood.* ANDREA *is to remove it from the hole as soon as the
sun comes out, so that the beam of light will illuminate . . . The stage
inside, now in shadow. The cameras are ready. In the darkness, a*
CHOREOGRAPHER *speaks in subdued tones to the* PRIMA
BALLERINA.

CHOREOGRAPHER: Movies are light. You're not on a stage, here.
> When the light hits your face, not from a light bulb, but
> natural, true sunlight . . . When you feel it, the audience has
> to feel it with you. Now get up, and take your places.

MABEL: The sun? Where's it gonna be coming from?

EDNA: I don't know . . .

CHOREOGRAPHER: From up above: there are two people in front
> of those panels.
> (*The sun is about to come out from behind the clouds.* NICOLA
> *looks at* ANDREA.)

NICOLA: Is it time?
> (ANDREA *is ready. The sun comes out.* ANDREA *removes the cover
> and light pours through the hole.*)

DIRECTOR: Roll it!
> (*The* PRIMA BALLERINA *is struck by a ray of sun and sweeps into
> movement. She is accompanied by gramophone music.* NICOLA
> *opens a big curtain. Sunlight pours into the room, showering the
> other dancers with light.* ANDREA *and* NICOLA *watch in
> enchantment, their eyes fixed on 'their' ballerinas.*)

36. EXT. BIRDHOUSE/WOODS. SUNSET

*The sun is setting behind the woods around the birdhouse. Shrieks of birds
come from the house, joining other birds hidden in the branches of trees.*

37. INT. BIRDHOUSE. SUNSET

His eyes filled with love, NICOLA *is reciting something quietly to
himself in Italian.*

NICOLA: '. . . air is the thing around your head, that becomes lighter when you laugh . . .'
(*Sitting in front of each other, the brothers write their love notes. The table is full of pieces of paper: some with writing, some without. The screaming of the birds is deafening as sunset approaches.* NICOLA *impatiently jumps to his feet and draws a black curtain in front of the birdcages.*)
Shut up! For you it's night!
(*Silence falls.* ANDREA *smiles to himself over a new phrase that has popped into his head, and he writes it on another piece of paper.* NICOLA *bends over his shoulder to read it.* ANDREA *reads it out loud.*)
ANDREA: 'You are as beautiful as a snowy mountain . . .'
(NICOLA *finishes it, intoning.*)
NICOLA: '. . . I'll put you in my shadow, to keep you from melting.'
(*The two brothers carefuly fold up the notes. They divide them in two groups. Then a doubt comes into their minds.*)
ANDREA: How are we going to deliver them?
(*A blackbird that has somehow managed to get out of its cage hops up and down on the table whistling. The brothers stare at it. They look at each other, struck by the same idea. Whistling like the blackbird,* ANDREA *makes a proposal to* NICOLA. NICOLA *understands him and whistles back.* ANDREA *picks up the blackbird's empty cage. The door is open. He stuffs his bunch of notes in the cage.* NICOLA *does the same with another cage.*)
Let's put them in two separate cages.
NICOLA: Good idea!
ANDREA: When? Where can we give these to them?
NICOLA: On the trolley?
ANDREA: Good!

38. INT. TROLLEY. MORNING
The streetcar is moving and MABEL *and* EDNA *stare at their strange gifts. On one cage is the name* EDNA, *written in red. On the other is* MABEL. *They open the doors, while the other passengers look on curiously. They pull out the little white notes. They start opening*

them. Looking over EDNA's *shoulder,* MARGA *reads the note out loud.*)

MARGA: 'Sometimes I fall into your eyes. Who knows where I'll end up?' Oh!
(*Shocked silence. Then there is an outburst of general mirth. Amused and curious, all the passengers start laughing.*)

LINDA: (*Laughing*) 'Fall into your eyes'?

MARGA: Oh no, we're all friends! Edna!

MARK: Oh, read another one!
(EDNA *hands* MARGA *another note.*)

MARGA: 'You're as beautiful as a snowy mountain . . .'
(*Close shot of* EDNA *and* MABEL. *Almost crushed by the crowd pushing up around them, they have remained sitting in their seats with the birdcages on their laps, listening with burning eyes to the words that are dedicated to them and them alone. Without realizing what they are doing, they finish the phrase with* MARGA.)
'. . . I'll put you in my shadow, to keep you from melting.'
(*The* CONDUCTOR, *who is almost driving to the sound of music, catches the phrase and savours it like a real connoisseur.*)

CONDUCTOR: (*Exclaiming in conclusion*) Shakespeare!
(*The love theme swells.*)

39. INT. DRUGSTORE. NIGHT

Almost to the sound of music, a SODA JERK *standing at the end of a long counter sends two marvellous ice-cream sundaes sliding toward the camera.*

SODA JERK: (*Shouting*) Two snowy mountains comin' up!
(*The sundaes slide into close up. Two little kids snatch them up.*)

40. EXT. HOLLYWOOD HILLS. DAY

The love theme swells around the top of a little hill where a CAMERAMAN *is tilting his camera up with the sky in the background. From either side of the hill appear two fine grey horses. The* CAMERAMAN *frowns.*

CAMERAMAN: They're the wrong colour. Get them out of here! I said white horses . . . White! White! Like two snowy mountains!

(From behind the hill appears a grinning young COWBOY, *leading two magnificent white horses by the bridle.)*

41. EXT. BABYLON SET. DAY

The sun and music grow in intensity. From the dark belly of a Sphinx, on top of a pyramid, appears D. W. GRIFFITH. *In the blinding sun he himself is dazzling, dressed in white from head to toe. The midday sun beats down on him, almost seeming to make him sway in its rays. He stops uncertainly at the top of the steps. A woman's voice calls out to him sweetly. It's his wife, who is climbing the steps of the pyramid towards him.*

MRS GRIFFITH: David! Watch out, you'll melt like a snowy
    mountain! Stay by me, come . . .
    *(She joins him and lovingly offers him the protection of her
    white umbrella.)*
    Let me keep you in my shadow . . .
    *(*GRIFFITH *presses himself to her, looking astonished and
    affectionate.)*
GRIFFITH: 'Keep you in my shadow'?
MRS GRIFFITH: Yes.
GRIFFITH: Are we speaking in verse today, my dear?

42. EXT. STUDIO YARD. DAY

Another model elephant is destroyed. ANDREA *and* NICOLA *smash it to pieces with sledgehammers.*

43. INT. MABEL'S AND EDNA'S APARTMENT. DAY

Close-up of one of the brothers' notes.

MABEL: *(Voice over)* 'Andrea and Nicola invite Edna and Mabel
    to lunch tomorrow in the birdhouse.'
    *(The table is covered with love notes. One of them is the
    invitation to dinner.* EDNA's *hand comes into frame. She runs
    her fingers over it caressingly for a second. Suddenly* MABEL's
    hand sweeps everything off the table, with untoward force.)*
    (Voice over) Remember what we promised each other? We'll
    only go out with . . .
    *(*EDNA *and* MABEL *are standing beside the table. They're in
    their underwear. They avoid each other's gaze. For a few*

seconds they just stand there in silence. Then each tries to justify
herself to the other.)
EDNA: Directors or producers.
MABEL: Yeah . . . What a lotta laughs.
(EDNA *looks out of the window.*)

44. EXT. STREET. DAY
*Two men in an automobile drive up outside the house. They get out
and wait in the street.*
EDNA: (*Voice over*) They're here. Mr Grass and company, right
on the dot.
MABEL: (*Voice over*) Listen, what if we ask them for a
raincheck? We can still get to the woods on time.
EDNA: (*Voice over*) Forget it, Mabel. Getting involved with
Nicola and Andrea would be like building houses on
quicksand. Those two are losers.

45. INT. MABEL'S AND EDNA'S APARTMENT. DAY
MABEL: Poor guys, we're late.

EDNA: Oh, let them wait.
  (*The two girls move away from the table to finish dressing.*
  EDNA *looks into a mirror.*)
  Oh, look at those lips! Whenever they chap like that, I just
  know something's gonna go wrong.
MABEL: Let me tell you, the best medicine is to laugh.
  (*As the girls start putting on their blouses, the sound of the horn
  from Mr Grass's car comes from outside.*)

46. EXT. NEAR THE BIRDHOUSE. DAY

Two splendid cups of lemon ice, white as two snowy mountains.
Melting. A rickety table has been set in front of the birdhouse. Set for
four; with unmatched but gay plates and utensils. In the middle are
the two white ices. Sitting at the ends of the table are ANDREA *and*
NICOLA, *silent and gloomy. They've been waiting for two hours. In*
vain. With a sudden burst of violence NICOLA *sweeps the ices off the*
table, which noisily roll off on the side. Once again there is silence.
Nothing moves. Then ANDREA *speaks in a distant, almost toneless*
voice.

ANDREA: I wish I wasn't here.
> (*His words send shivers up and down* NICOLA's *spine.*)

NICOLA: We have the money to go back.
> (*He gets up and opens a trunk. He pulls out a pair of cymbals and then a wad of dollar bills, tied with a red ribbon. He flips through them.*)

ANDREA: Yes, but just enough to go back. What would we tell Babbo?
> (ANDREA *picks up one of the cymbals and hits it.*)

I wish I was back home in the square, playing with the band.
> (NICOLA *stands up and starts clearing the table. He takes the things inside.*)

47. INT. BIRDHOUSE. DAY
NICOLA *opens the birdcage. He distributes the uneaten food to the birds.*
NICOLA: What will we do now, huh?

48. EXT. BIRDHOUSE. DAY
ANDREA *walks into the forest, carrying the cymbals.* NICOLA *returns from the birdhouse and sits down at the table, looking blankly in front of him. The sound of a cymbal crash.*

49. EXT. FOREST. DAY
ANDREA *is standing by a stream crashing the cymbals together. In front of him is a music stand which holds the score of Rossini's* La Gazza Ladra. *The camera moves across the notes of the score. The sound of the cymbals continues – at first on its own. Gradually the full score is heard.*

50. INT. BONANNO'S FARMHOUSE KITCHEN. NIGHT
The mysterious sound of those cymbals reaches even old BONANNO. *Like* NICOLA *he is sitting in front of an empty table in a big country kitchen. He stares at . . . a glass of red wine standing in the middle of the table. The old man's hand comes into frame, picks up the glass, and brings it to his mouth. He drinks.*

61

51. EXT. NEAR THE BIRDHOUSE. DAY

Still sitting at the table, alone, NICOLA *stares at a glass of wine –
harder and harder. The wine glass magically begins to slide towards
him. Or maybe it's only his imagination. Then, however,* NICOLA
*picks it up with a knowing nod and takes a sip. He drinks, watching
an image grow clearer and clearer.*

52. EXT. FOREST. DAY

ANDREA *seems to be seeing the same image. The image takes form: it
is the marvellous white elephant of the Cathedral of San Michele.
The two brothers are putting on the final touches. Close shot of the
elephant. Its whiteness glows with pure light. Close shot of the forest
ground. With sticks the brothers' hands are tracing the shape of an
elephant: rearing up, with its trunk raised.*

ANDREA: (*Voice over*) This is the elephant Griffith has been
    waiting for!

NICOLA: (*Voice over*) We'll build one for him standing up . . .
    Life-size!

53. EXT. CLEARING IN THE WOODS. DAY

In the middle of the woods is a natural circular clearing. The brothers plant a wooden pole in the middle of it; around it they'll build the elephant. Dissolve to –

54. EXT. CLEARING IN THE WOODS. DAY

The wooden sub-structure of the elephant is taking shape.

55. EXT. HOLLYWOOD STREET. NIGHT

Like two burglars, the brothers tear movie posters off the walls.

56. EXT. CLEARING IN THE WOODS. DAY

The clearing is a festival of colours, faces and writing from movie posters. ANDREA *stirs the poster paper around in a big tub, to turn it into papier mâché.* NICOLA *is modelling one of the elephant's legs out of the mixture. Dissolve to – In the middle of the clearing, the elephant is beginning to assume its final form, created out of the thousand colours of papier mâché.* ANDREA *stands on top of a ladder, modelling the giant trunk raised in the air.* NICOLA *hands him tools from the ground. Dissolve to –*

57. EXT. CLEARING IN THE WOODS. NIGHT

A rainstorm. The two brothers desperately try to protect the elephant from the rain. Dissolve to –

58. EXT. CLEARING IN THE WOODS. DAY

The storm is over. The elephant is still standing. The brothers plunge into their work again with desperate tenacity. Dissolve to – The elephant is being painted grey. Its trunk resembles a sword thrust into the sky. Dissolve to –

59. EXT. CLEARING IN THE WOODS. MORNING

It is Sunday morning, and the elephant is finished. Deep silence reigns around it: the animated silence of morning woods. The camera slowly backs away, revealing two silent figures standing on the edge of the clearing: MABEL *and* EDNA.

EDNA: Did they build that?

MABEL: No, I can't believe it . . . It's too beautiful.

(*They admire the elephant in awe. They try to understand it. Timidly they approach the creature, walk around it. And there, with their arms thrown around each other, lie* NICOLA *and* ANDREA, *fast asleep between the feet of their masterpiece. Their faces are lined with fatigue, but from inside them shines an almost childlike tranquillity.* MABEL *and* EDNA *stare at them with painful tenderness. Dissolve to – The sun is high over the trees now, and the camera slowly approaches a part of the woods that is secluded and grassy. On the ground are the figures of two young people making love. They are* EDNA *and* NICOLA. EDNA *lets his excited hands lower the top of her slip revealing her breasts. He throws himself forward to kiss her.* EDNA *pulls away from him, looking a little confused.*)

EDNA: What are you doing? Are you going to undress?
NICOLA: I took off my vest!
    (EDNA *cuddles up to his fully clothed body.*)
EDNA: But a person wants to smell the skin.
NICOLA: I know, but I'm ashamed.
EDNA: What about me, then?

(*Now* EDNA *seems to feel ashamed of her own nudity and tries to cover her burgeoning breasts with her hand.*)

NICOLA: A woman's body is always beautiful.

EDNA: At least your boots!

(EDNA *bends over to untie* NICOLA's *boots. She slips the first one off. A foot appears in a sock full of holes.* NICOLA *bends over to hide the holes with his hand.*)

NICOLA: (*Exclaiming*) I . . . I told you!

(*They burst out laughing. The camera leaves them and slowly starts moving through the woods again. While the laughter of the two lovers grows more distant the camera moves in on an even more secluded corner of the woods, revealing another couple lying on the grass. This time it is* ANDREA *and* MABEL. ANDREA *is kissing* MABEL's *foot. They embrace and kiss. Suddenly* MABEL *draws away from* ANDREA's *arms. She stares into his eyes, suddenly struck by something. Like every lover, she seems to want to penetrate her beloved's heart with her gaze.*)

MABEL: (*Murmuring*) It's good to be with you, Andrea . . .

(*She has a strange hesitation. Then she laughs with a little quiver in her voice.*)

Even if sometimes I feel like I'm with two people . . . you know?

(ANDREA *doesn't understand. But, like every lover, he wants to understand. He raises himself up on his elbows, quizzically.*)

Edna and me, I mean, we're friends too, but it's different . . . with you there's something more. You two are always together, the same . . . Always equal to each other.

(ANDREA *has stopped smiling. He stares at her a long time.*)

ANDREA: No . . . We are both . . .

(*He thinks the better of it and is silent.* MABEL *senses he's holding back.*)

MABEL: No. Tell me what you were about to say.

(ANDREA *lets himself fall back on the grass. He seems lost in thought.* MABEL *squeezes his hand hard.*)

Please – Tell me.

(*When* ANDREA *starts to speak, the echo of distant distress reverberates in his voice.*)

ANDREA: I was thinking about one time when Nicola and I were

65

not equal, as you say. We were about nine and ten and we each had two cents in our pockets . . . We bought a ticket apiece. Nicola got number eighteen, I got fifty. Come here. (MABEL *moves closer to* ANDREA.)
Eighteen came out. Nicola won this beautiful Spanish knife.

60. EXT. STREET. DAY

ANDREA *and* NICOLA *are seen as young boys in the shadow of the ancient walls of the city where they grew up.* NICOLA *lifts the knife up in the air in a sign of victory.*

ANDREA: (*Voice over*) Chance had favoured just one of us: our strength, our equality had been destroyed.
(*With self-satisfied generosity* NICOLA *turns to his brother.* ANDREA *brushes aside his brother's hand which is holding the knife for him to see. It is such a violent, brutal gesture that* NICOLA *bites his lip angrily at the insult. The two boys suddenly hurl themselves at each other. They punch each other and roll over the ground. They are overcome with fury, exasperation, hatred; it is wordless and reciprocal. Everything the one couldn't stand in the other, and that remained buried deep inside him for years under their daily exchanges of affection and common interests, explodes with murderous fury now that chance has unbalanced their equality. The knife strikes the back of* ANDREA's *hand. A rivulet of blood appears. For a second, hypnotized by the red blood, the brothers stop fighting and face each other, panting. Then they go for each other again, with redoubled fury. It is a fight with no way out.* ANDREA *grabs the knife from where it has fallen on the ground. The knife gashes* NICOLA's *forehead. A rivulet of blood appears. The knife falls to the ground. The two brothers gaze at it, bleeding. They look at each other – stalemate.*)

61. EXT. WOODS. DAY

ANDREA *has now finished his story. His eyes are closed, his arm raised as though he was still clutching the knife.* MABEL *shivers on the cold grass.*

MABEL: Why tell me this story? To scare me?

66

(ANDREA *opens his eyes. He struggles back to reality. With infinite tenderness he gazes at* MABEL *and shakes his head.*)

ANDREA: No – to make you realize how much you mean to me. You're the first person I've told it to.

(MABEL *takes* ANDREA's *hand in hers and attempts to kiss it.* ANDREA *smiles and indicates his other hand.*)

The scar is over here.

(MABEL *kisses the spot where the knife wound has left a scar. On the other side of the woods, where the other couple has made its nest,* EDNA *points with a questioning look at the scar on* NICOLA's *forehead.*)

EDNA: Is this the scar?

(NICOLA *nods.*)

Nicky!

NICOLA: Yes, but don't tell Andrea I've told you this story, my love. He'd never forgive me.

(EDNA *reaches out and brushes the scar on* NICOLA's *forehead with her fingertips. As though he had received an electric shock,* NICOLA *grabs her hand and with sudden, terrible violence, pushes it away from him, squeezing till it hurts. Frightened but rebellious,* EDNA *pulls her hand away. The flash of hatred, with its ancient roots, dies out of* NICOLA's *face. Once more burning with love, he takes the woman's hand in his and brings it to his forehead. He puts it there, as though asking to be forgiven, and to receive reassurance. Fade out.*)

62. EXT. CLEARING IN THE WOODS. NIGHT

It is night and the woods are drenched in moonlight. Down in the circular clearing, in front of the elephant, a fire has been lit. Around it, like an ancient tribe, sit the two brothers, their women and their friends.

ANDREA: (*Voice over*) Those were happy days. Edna and Mabel introduced us to their friends, people from all over the world who had come to work in the movies.

NICOLA: (*Voice over*) One evening they came to see us, and we took them to see our elephant. Was it worthy of being shown to Griffith?

THOMPSON: It's a little grey, isn't it?

67

NICOLA: An elephant is grey.

STEVE: It's true to reality, but it won't stand out on film.

SEAN: If it was light, Andrea, I'd shoot some test footage. Then
you'd see.

STEVE: Yeah, right.

(MABEL *looks up at her man, looks at the elephant, looks at the
sky.*)

MABEL: It'll be day soon . . . in a couple of hours! Why don't we
wait for dawn?

(*Some of their friends who have overheard her look around
uncertainly.* EDNA *gives a glad shout.*)

EDNA: Oh, yeah! Let's wait! Please, Sean! I never saw the sun
come up in the woods before.

SEAN: Listen, if I'm going to shoot this thing, I want it perfect.
So who's going to give me a hand to whitewash this monster?

MARGA: All of us.

ANDREA: Hey, listen. Let's make a circle of candles around him.

MARK: What?

ANDREA: A circle of candles around the elephant!

68

(The group place their candles in a circle around the elephant and ladders are set up as they prepare to whitewash the elephant.)

63. EXT. CLEARING IN THE WOODS. DAWN

The black of night has given way to the rosy pinks of dawn. The sun is coming up over the woods. A quiver runs through the treetops. In the clearing everyone is on their feet, cold and shivering, clinging to each other in twos. Some have a blanket wrapped around them. Almost all of them have splotches of whitewash on their hands, faces and clothes. MARGA *passes among the group pouring wine.*

STEVE: How's the light, OK?

SEAN: Yeah, just about.

> *(The sound of sobbing is heard. It's* EDNA. *Her voice is strange. Everyone looks in her direction. Ashamed of her sobs,* EDNA *tries to excuse herself.)*

EDNA: Oh . . . oh, I'm sorry folks. I guess I overdid the drink a little. Just what I wanted to say is . . . Anyhow, who knows where we'll be ten, twenty years from now! Just let's promise never to forget the way we are now, together, and how we're helping each other. Oh dear, I'm . . . what . . . what . . . I mean is, that's why the movies, for me – this Hollywood of ours – is so wonderful. Because you – I mean . . . we –

> *(She nods at the group of friends now sitting together around the elephant made by* ANDREA *and* NICOLA, *then she breaks off almost angrily.)*

Oh, isn't it light enough yet?

> *(She hides her face, red with embarrassment, crying and laughing.)*

NICOLA: Is it time?

SEAN: Yes.

> *(The first ray of sun cuts through the leaden sky. The cameraman,* SEAN, *begins filming the elephant, which now appears in the first rays of sun a blinding new white. The camera rolls.* SEAN *senses someone beside him. He stops and turns. It's* ANDREA. *The cameraman gives him a questioning look and* ANDREA *nods. Then* SEAN *steps down from the camera and* ANDREA *takes his place. He peers through the lens.*

69

*And he films his elephant. Then, without turning around, he too
steps down. He moves aside, leaving his place to* NICOLA, *who
gets up to the camera and looks through the eyepiece. He shoots.
Close shot of elephant. Fade out.*)

64. EXT. CLEARING IN THE WOODS. DAY
*It is full day, and nobody is left in the clearing. Only the elephant
remains standing in the middle. Yet there is someone: behind the
trees, a man stands still, looking. It is* GRASS. *He looks at the
elephant with an expression that is half incredulous, half ferocious.
Three of his trusted assistants arrive from various parts of the woods.
They approach the elephant in amazement. They circle around it.
One of them, almost as though he couldn't believe his eyes, touches it
with his fingertip. He pulls it back like it was fire: the elephant is
real, all right. The first assistant goes up to* GRASS. *He refers to the
elephant, in conclusion.*
DIEGO: Those two dagos!
    (*A third man cackles sycophantically to* GRASS.)
TOM: A flop!

70

(GRASS *gives him a contemptuous look.*)

GRASS: It's a masterpiece. A masterpiece!

(*The assistant is left speechless. He gulps.*)

DIEGO: (*Murmuring*) Shall we take it to Mr Griffith?

(GRASS *gives him another look of contempt and doesn't deign to answer. He takes a few steps in the direction of the elephant. He pulls out a cigar, and strikes a match. But instead of lighting his cigar, he lights his newspaper. The assistant watches open-mouthed. Then he finally understands. As exhilarated as only the stupid can be, he lights a match in turn. The elephant is surrounded by a wall of flame. Only now does* GRASS *light his cigar. The elephant has become a blazing bonfire. Dissolve to —*

65. EXT. SET OF INTOLERANCE UNDER CONSTRUCTION. DAY
Gloomy and homicidal, the two brothers march across the unfinished set of Intolerance. *They seem to see nothing, hear nothing and no one.*
NICOLA *sees what he's after. He goes up to* GRASS, *who is supervising the work.* DIEGO *is holding chains in his hand.*

DIEGO: They're not made of iron . . . If you pull on 'em, you'll break them.

GRASS: Tom, we've got to change all the brown tiles, they're too light . . . Put in darker ones . . . all the way up . . .

TOM: OK.

GRASS: (*Seeing* NICOLA *approaching*) You . . .

(NICOLA *plants himself squarely in front of* GRASS *and slaps him in the face.* GRASS *staggers; he instinctively takes a couple of steps backwards but finds himself facing the other brother,* ANDREA, *who sends him back to where he was with another terrifying slap.* EDNA *and* MABEL *pull the brothers away from* GRASS.)

EDNA: You want to ruin yourselves?

MABEL: This is just what Grass wants. Stop it!

EDNA: Nicky! He'll throw you out of here for good.

(TOM *calls to the extras dressed as Babylonian guards.*)

TOM: Hey, you guys, give me a hand!

(*The guards form a barrier protecting* GRASS. *The brothers throw themselves at* GRASS *once again, but are overwhelmed by the guards and Grass's assistants. At the same time, the extras are holding back* MABEL *and* EDNA.)

71

MABEL: Let me go, let me go! Leave me alone!

EDNA: (*To* THOMPSON) Do something!

THOMPSON: Don't worry . . .

  (*The brothers, tied up in the chains, are being held by the Babylonian guards.*)

TOM: You wanted to work in movies, didn't you? We never tested these chains before . . . They seem to hold up.

GRASS: We're just testing the chains for the slave scene!

THOMPSON: (*Trying to mediate*) Come on, take them off!

GRASS: Thompson, you take yourself off this set!

FIRST GUARD: (*Moving the two brothers off the set*) Let's go.

SECOND GUARD: Move it.

66. EXT. GAOL. EVENING

The gloomy outside of the gaol. A Black Maria pulls up in front of the huge iron gate. From the van appear two POLICE OFFICERS, *who hustle* ANDREA *and* NICOLA *out of the back. They're handcuffed. The gate opens in front of them. They are shoved inside. The gaol swallows them up behind the closing gate: the big iron gate*

*slamming shut. For ever, it would seem. And yet, at a certain
moment, something mysterious starts to move, something that seems to
go right through the gate, break it down, dissolve it in a radiance that
little by little assumes a form and a definite outline: that of an
elephant standing on its hind legs, with its trunk raised in the air – a
white elephant – or rather, a black and white elephant . . .*

67. INT. SCREENING ROOM. DAY
*On the screen of Griffith's studio room, the image of the elephant
appears in gigantic proportions: the elephant filmed at dawn in the
woods by* SEAN *and the two brothers. The room. Sitting in front of
the screen, seen from behind, wearing his usual wide-brimmed hat, is*
D. W. GRIFFITH. *The film is rolling in front of him: the elephant
from the front, the sides, from overhead, from ground level, in
detail . . . Its raised trunk looks like a white blade against the sky.
Hidden behind the glass inside the projection booth,* MABEL *and*
EDNA, *along with* SEAN *and projectionist* STEVE *watch the film with
their hearts in their throats. It is they who have brought* GRIFFITH
the film. Now they have to hastily duck to keep from being seen. The

lights go on in the screening room. Slowly SEAN *lifts his head until only his eyes are visible, to see what's going on.*

SEAN: Is he looking at it, huh?

STEVE: Yeah.

> (*From overhead, as though from the projection booth:* GRIFFITH, *still seen from behind, sits in silence a few seconds. Then he stands up.*)

GRIFFITH: I want eight of those elephants. They're wonderful!

THOMPSON: (*Looking embarrassed*) But the two Italian guys that made it have gone away . . .

GRIFFITH: Gone where?

THOMPSON: To gaol.

GRIFFITH: You're kidding. What did they do?

THOMPSON: They got in a fight . . .

GRIFFITH: With whom?

> (THOMPSON *doesn't have the courage to tell him and shrugs his shoulders. But from behind* GRIFFITH *someone answers the question. It's* GRIFFITH's *wife, as sweetly ironic as ever.*)

MRS GRIFFITH: Ask me. With your production man.

GRIFFITH: Grass?

> (GRIFFITH *turns to his wife and finally shows his face, which has broken into the merriest, most youthful peals of laughter.*) Grass!!
> (*The news seems to amuse him no end.*)
> Then get those two delinquents out on bail at once, and bring them to me!
> (*In the projection booth, it is a tender moment of victory. The two women quietly thank* SEAN *and the projectionist.*)

68. EXT. STUDIO. DAY

EDNA *and* MABEL *burst out of the projection room, running with joy.*

69. INT. CORRIDOR. DAY

The long studio corridor. MABEL *and* EDNA *run towards the end of it. In the middle of the hall a* CLEANING WOMAN *is washing the floor with two buckets. The two girls don't even slow down and leap together over the pails, with the elevation of real ballerinas. And like ballerinas, they come down gracefully and go on running down the hall.*

70. EXT. INTOLERANCE SET UNDER CONSTRUCTION. DAY
The music swells up. The whole ballet corps is whirling around in a dance. On the steps of the set a rehearsal is in progress for the Babylonian dance scene. The dancing girls are already in costume. MABEL *and* EDNA *dance forward with their line, their faces happy and serious.*

71. INT. BONANNO BROS OFFICE. DAY
Dressed and spruced up like a pair of studio execs, the brothers stand in front of two enormous desks. NICOLA *points to the right-hand desk.*

NICOLA: This is mine. That's yours.
ANDREA: Sure, they're the same . . . I'd feel funny sitting
    behind a desk like this.
    (*The two brothers sit on the chairs* in front *of the desks.*)
NICOLA: Me, too. If our father could see us now.
ANDREA: No, we can bring him over.
    (*There is a knock at the door.* NICOLA *starts to call for the person to come in, but* ANDREA *stops him.*)
    No . . . Wait a moment!
    (*The two brothers quickly go round behind their desks and sit down.* GRASS *enters the office with a sheaf of papers in his hand.*)
    Who tol– . . . Who told you to come in?
GRASS: I knocked . . .
NICOLA: Were you in the service?
GRASS: Sure . . .
ANDREA: Then about face! Forward march! Hup–two,
    hup–two, hup . . .
    (GRASS *pauses. The expression on his face shows that he realizes that the power has now shifted.*)
ANDREA and NICOLA (*Louder*) Hup–two, hup–two, hup–two,
    hup–two, hup–two, hup–two, hup–two, hup–two . . .
    (GRASS *turns on his heel and marches out.* MABEL, EDNA *and some of the other dancers have been watching through the*

window. Laughing at GRASS's *humiliation,* MABEL *turns to the other dancers.*)

MABEL: About face! Forward, march! Hup–two, hup–two, hup–two . . .

EDNA: Hup–two, hup–two, hup–two, hup–two, hup–two, hup–two, hup–two, hup–two!

(EDNA, MABEL, *and the dancers start marching. Their hilarity is contagious. The other dancing girls, who have finished the Babylonian ballet rehearsal, improvise a wild, brazen, modern dance. Other young people who were working on the set, white and black, join in the dance, which gets faster and faster. The music swells. Dissolve to* –

72. EXT. BABYLON SET. DAY

The orchestra is playing on the vast lot where the Babylon set of Intolerance *has been finally finished in all its grandeur. In the middle, giant, white and splendid, are eight elephants. They stand on their hind legs with their trunks raised in the air, on top of the mammoth columns of Belshazzar's palace. Beneath the elephants a long table has been laid for the wedding banquet. The last hurried touches are given: flowers, drinks, seats. Bustling about at these activities are the couples' friends, all dressed up for the occasion:* MARGA, SEAN *and* THOMPSON *are the most active.* THOMPSON *and* MARGA *lug two extra-large chairs over.*

THOMPSON: Are these for the bride and groom?

MARGA: No, for Mr Griffith and Bonanni . . .

SEAN: (*Remembering*) Mr Bonanni, right . . .

MARGA: They wanted their father to be here, too.

THOMPSON: We have important guests today . . .

MARGA: (*With affection and admiration*) Oh, Mr Griffith loves those boys; they're the apple of his eye.

(*A* COOK *in a big hat is arranging a tray of fruit. He turns to his* ASSISTANT.)

COOK: Who is this Italian father, anyway?

ASSISTANT: Some big artist from Tuscany.

COOK: What's his name?

ASSISTANT: Michelangelo . . . or Raphael . . .

COOK: Raphael? Yeah, I heard of him. I thought he was dead.

(*Everyone's attention is now drawn to the stage door.*)

MARGA: Here they come.

(*On the other side of the constructions, three huge automobiles are pulling up. The two brides and grooms get out, and hurry to the third car. Out of it steps old* BONANNO. *The years of waiting have left their mark on his face.* EDNA *and* MABEL *help* BONANNO *out of the car.*)

BONANNO: Thank you.

ANDREA: (*Indicating the set of* Intolerance) Do you like it?

BONANNO: Yes, it's beautiful . . .

NICOLA: This is our studio . . .

ANDREA: Let's go . . .

NICOLA: Come . . .

ANDREA: The wedding feast is being offered by our master, D. W. Griffith.

(*From the back of the studio comes* GRIFFITH. *He speaks to two of his assistants, then starts moving alone towards the wedding group.*)

NICOLA: Here he is. He's coming to greet you.

(*Old* BONANNO *takes a look at* GRIFFITH *and starts towards him with* ANDREA *and* NICOLA *at his side. After three steps he stops, struck by an idea. He points to a cane lying on the ground.*)

BONANNO: Give me that cane. I'll go on alone.

(*Limping slightly with the cane,* BONANNO *goes towards* GRIFFITH. *The two brothers put their arms around their wives.*)

EDNA: I never noticed he limped.

NICOLA: He does it on purpose.

MABEL: On purpose?

ANDREA: He wants to seem even older.

(BONANNO *and* GRIFFITH *come to a halt, a few paces from each other, in the middle of the set.*)

NICOLA: Which is going to greet the other first?

(*A long silence.* BONANNO *lets the cane slip to the ground. He starts to bend to pick it up.* GRIFFITH *gestures for him to stop, then picks up the cane and gives it to* BONANNO.)

BONANNO: Good morning, maestro.

GRIFFITH: Good morning.
(*The two men bow to each other. Cut to: the wedding table in front of the* Intolerance *set. All the guests are seated round the table enjoying themselves.* GRIFFITH *raises his voice and asks:*)
May I make so bold as to ask your age, sir?
(*The question is translated to the old man.*)
MARGA: (*In Italian*) How old are you?
(BONANNO *doesn't hesitate.*)
BONANNO: Novanta.
MARGA: Ninety!
(*The brothers' smiles fade and they blush, looking down.*)
ANDREA: Papa!
NICOLA: Ninety . . . He's seventy!
(*The old man gets up with ostentatious difficulty. He asks for silence with a gesture. He gets it.* BONANNO *raises both hands to his breast and then over his head, in his gesture of blessing.*)
YOUNG MAN: Hey, what's he doing?
BONANNO: This is the way our ancestors gave their blessing. And it's for you, Mabel, and for you, Edna.
EDNA: It's for us, he said?
BONANNO: And for you two sons of mine.
THOMPSON: (*To* GRIFFITH *and* MRS GRIFFITH) It's a traditional blessing. It's for Mabel and Edna, and, of course, for the sons.
(BONANNO *sits down again. The orchestra strikes up once more. But* BONANNO *immediately gets to his feet and again silences the orchestra.*)
BONANNO: Maybe this is mean of me, but I have to tell the truth. I blessed my two sons, I shouldn't have. You didn't keep your promise. You left in order to return. You worked on foreign soil to be able to continue on your own soil, the work of your father, and the father of your father, and on back to the ancestors who built our cathedrals. Useless years have passed while this old man waited for his sons to keep their promise.
(*The table has fallen silent. Everyone's eyes are on the brothers. Pale and excited, they want to say something, and each encourages the other.* NICOLA *stands up.*)

79

NICOLA: Devo . . .

> (*Unable to continue, he sits down.* ANDREA *rises, attempts to say something, but cannot find the words. Then* ANDREA *sits down and, like* NICOLA, *bows his head.* D. W. GRIFFITH *gets to his feet and starts to speak.*)

GRIFFITH: Maybe it's not my place to speak: I am not a son or a relative, nor have I ninety summers on my head like you, Signor Bonanno, but like you I'm used to saying what I think. Now, I . . . I do not know whether our work, that of your sons and mine, is as fine as that of those who built the Romanesque cathedrals. I do know that those works were born as these are born today – of the same collective dream. I believe that your sons, Bonanni, are like those obscure stone-cutters who carved their masterpieces on the cathedrals you honour, who contributed to making them famous with their art, and who helped their neighbour to believe and live better.

> (*The faces of those gathered around the wedding table, each in its own way, express agreement and resolution, humility and pride, but above all astonishment at recognizing a simple truth, which only now becomes conscious.* GRIFFITH *concludes:*)

This is why I love movie-making and I respect it, Bonnani.

> (*A deeply moved silence has fallen over the table, surrounded by all that ridiculous Babylonian architecture. But not for long. It is* GRIFFITH *who breaks the spell he himself has woven.*)

You can tell I used to be an actor, eh? I've done a bit of everything in my life! (*Laughing*) But never have I given a better performance than today! Ladies and gentlemen . . .

> (GRIFFITH *offers a toast to the married couples. The orchestra strikes up again. All rise and drink in honour of the two couples.*)

73. MONTAGE OF NEWSPAPER HEADLINES
EUROPE AT WAR IN EUROPE; WILL AMERICA INTERVENE?; PROTESTS FEARED AT PREMIÈRE OF 'INTOLERANCE'; A FILM AGAINST WAR.

74. EXT. MOVIE THEATRE ENTRANCE. NIGHT
Bright lights, a swarm of people: it is the opening night of Intolerance. *The stars and makers of the film climb up the long flight of stairs*

between two rows of curious public. NICOLA *and* ANDREA *climb the stairs, too, with their wives. The camera frames* EDNA's *and* MABEL's *bellies, which they nonchalantly and joyously display in their eight months' glory. Dissolve to: the grandeur of the Babylonian sequence flickers on the screen; the white elephants trumpet triumphantly on top of the ninety-foot columns. A gasp of amazement and admiration rises up from the audience. In a box,* NICOLA *and* ANDREA *look at each other in pride.*

ANDREA: The elephants!

> (*One of the giant pachyderms appears in close shot on the screen on top of its column. Thunderous applause is heard. In the box below theirs, several enthusiastic viewers make comments.*)

WOMAN IN AUDIENCE: How tall do you think they are?

MAN IN AUDIENCE: The elephants?

> (NICOLA *leans over and answers the question.*)

NICOLA: The columns are ninety feet high, the elephants fifty.

> (ANDREA's *head pops out over his brother's shoulder. He can't resist boasting.*)

ANDREA: They weigh five tons each.

> (*Dissolve to: the orchestra seats. The lights go on in the theatre: the film is over.* GRIFFITH *thanks the applauding audience. With a sweep of his arm he includes the people who worked on the picture in the applause. Over the applause we hear people shouting congratulations, as well as slogans against the war. During the applause* GRIFFITH *gestures to the two brothers. The spotlight moves to them. They stand up with* EDNA *and* MABEL, *receiving the applause, with thanks. Dissolve to: the long staircase leading up to the theatre. The public pours out of the doors. If the atmosphere inside is excited, it's even more confused here, outside. Our two couples come out with the rest of the crowd. Suddenly they're buried under a storm of multi-coloured flyers, supporting the war. But* NICOLA *grabs one of the flyers and reads it. He turns serious. He shows it to his brother. On the flyer is written* AMERICANS TO JOIN THE WAR. ANDREA *looks up. On the balcony above the entrance a group of enthusiastic young men are throwing flyers into the air, while several hawkers are passing out newspapers and shouting the latest, dramatic news from the war in Europe. The crowd is*

82

growing restless. Policemen are trying to push people back from the entrance. An excited group of interventionists elbow their way furiously through the milling throng. Waving an American flag they climb a lamp post. Dismay, enthusiasm, astonishment sweep through the crowd in the confusion. MABEL *and* EDNA *get separated from their husbands. Suddenly* MABEL *stumbles and goes rolling down the stairs.* EDNA *fearfully rushes to her friend to help her, but is forced back by the pressure of the crowd.* MABEL *is lying motionless at the foot of the stairs. Like waves in a stormy sea, the crowd keeps pushing* EDNA *back. Her face is ashen and her eyes stricken with terror.* ANDREA *and* NICOLA *push their way through and rush down the stairs.* ANDREA *lifts up* MABEL. *Now and then she gives a moan or a stifled cry, pressing her hand to her belly.* NICOLA *races off to hail a taxi. When one arrives he helps* MABEL *and* ANDREA *into it. When the taxi departs, he and* EDNA *get into the next one.*

75. INT. ANDREA'S AND MABEL'S TAXI. NIGHT
TAXI DRIVER: (*Voice over*) Where to?
MABEL: Home, please.
TAXI DRIVER: (*Voice over*) Where's that? The address?
ANDREA: No, the hospital!

76. INT. NICOLA'S AND EDNA'S TAXI. NIGHT
NICOLA: Don't lose them! Go faster!
EDNA: Don't laugh, but I don't think I feel too well either.
NICOLA: What is it?
    (EDNA *moves into* NICOLA'S *arms.*)

77. INT. HOSPITAL CORRIDOR. NIGHT
MARGA *enters from Mabel's room with a baby in her arms.*
MARGA: Andrea . . .
    (ANDREA, NICOLA, THOMPSON *and* SEAN *move towards the baby.* ANDREA *takes his son in his arms.*)
NICOLA: Ciao.
THOMPSON: Why, he's a chip off the old block!
    (*The* DOCTOR *comes out of an adjoining room.* NICOLA *stops him.*)

NICOLA: Doctor! I'm the husband of the other lady. How much longer is there to wait?

DOCTOR: The other . . . ? The other lady isn't in labour, at least not for the moment.

NICOLA: Why not? She has pains!

DOCTOR: Maybe . . . Sympathy . . .

NICOLA: What do you mean, 'sympathy'?

DOCTOR: They could be sympathy pains. It happens; she saw her friend and consequently . . . you understand?

NICOLA: What shall I do then, take her home?

DOCTOR: No, I want to be certain that it is sympathy. Otherwise, it could be a bit more serious.

(*The* DOCTOR *walks away from* NICOLA *down the corridor. In the other group,* MARGA *authoritatively takes the baby from its father's arms.* ANDREA *happily comes over to* NICOLA, *who has let the* DOCTOR *go. He takes* NICOLA'*s arm conspiratorily*.)

ANDREA: Nicola! Know what I'm going to call him? Babbo's name – Bonanno!

NICOLA: No, wait! I thought of it first!

ANDREA: Mine's already been born!

NICOLA: Well, mine'll be here in a few days!

ANDREA: You can have grandpa's name.

NICOLA: I like Babbo's. Let's draw for it.

(EDNA *is wheeled down the hall on a bed by two* NURSES. NICOLA *goes to her and squeezes her hand.* EDNA *makes him bend over her face. Her words come slowly, half laughing, half crying.*)

EDNA: Oh, Nicky, I'm so stupid! So stupid! What will people think of me!

NICOLA: No . . .

EDNA: They may be just sympathy pains, but they really hurt.

NICOLA: My Edna, always the actress.

(*Her mouth trembles with suffering. Her voice gets lower and more defenceless.*)

EDNA: Nicky.

NICOLA: What?

EDNA: I hurt so bad.

NICOLA: How bad?

(*Before* EDNA *has a chance to reply, she is taken into her room. As she is wheeled away from* NICOLA, *his hand passes over her stomach.*)

EDNA: Where's Mabel?

NURSE: Your friend is in the next room. Her bed is right on the other side of the wall.

(NICOLA *is left standing alone in the doorway.*)

ANDREA: Nicola.

(ANDREA *is given a bouquet of flowers.*)

Oh, thank you. (*To* NICOLA) Any news?

NICOLA: No, nothing yet.

ANDREA: So, come on, come into Mabel's room, let's celebrate.

NICOLA: No, later I will. I'm going to get a breath of fresh air . . . You're settled, but not me.

(NICOLA *starts to move away.*)

ANDREA: Hey, tomorrow it's Edna's turn.

(NICOLA *walks down the corridor.*)

78. INT. MABEL'S ROOM. NIGHT

With her back raised on pillows, MABEL *holds the baby to her breast. Exhausted but happy, she gazes at . . .* ANDREA, *who comes through the door and walks to the bed. He bends down over his wife and puts the flowers on the table beside her. He bends over his infant son and murmurs to him in a voice filled with conspiratorial mischief.*

ANDREA: Bonanno! Bo–nan–no!

> (ANDREA *looks away from the baby towards the empty doorway where* NICOLA *had been standing.*)

79. EXT. DESERTED AREA BY THE SEA. NIGHT

NICOLA *is standing looking out to sea, restless and agitated. He goes and sits down on an empty bench.*

80. INT. HOSPITAL CORRIDOR. NIGHT

A NURSE *is sitting at the end of the empty corridor. Suddenly cries start coming from Edna's room. As* EDNA *begins shouting for* MABEL, *the nurse gets up and moves quickly towards Edna's room.*

81. INT. MABEL'S ROOM. NIGHT

MABEL: (*Banging on the wall*) Edna!

82. INT. EDNA'S ROOM. NIGHT

The light comes on, revealing EDNA's *pain-stricken face.*

EDNA: I'm dying!

> (*Dissolve to –*)

83. INT. HOSPITAL STAIRCASE. DAY

The light of dawn pours through the large hospital windows. NICOLA *climbs the stairs. At the top of the stairs the ashen, silent faces of* ANDREA, THOMPSON *and* SEAN *are waiting for him. The group at the top is silent.* NICOLA *realizes it's all over. He looks at them. He looks at* ANDREA *as though he didn't recognize him and a strange voice comes out of his throat.*

NICOLA: What a pretty picture!

> (*He pushes them aside.*)

NICOLA *enters and stares at his dead wife. He asks a question between desperation and terror.*

NICOLA: What have you done?
  (ANDREA's *hand comes down on* NICOLA's *shoulder in pity. Suddenly* NICOLA *shakes it off, shivering.*)
  Don't touch me!
  (*He takes a step backward and finds himself in front of* MARGA. *Next to* MARGA *is* NICOLA's *child. He seems not to understand.*)

MARGA: Nicola . . .

NICOLA: What is this doing here?

MARGA: He's . . . he's your son, Nicola.
  (*He looks at the baby. Then at his dead wife. He understands.*)

ANDREA: Don't worry about him. Mabel will just have two sons, instead of one. She'll nurse yours too. She'll take care of you as she does me.
  (NICOLA *doesn't answer. It's almost as though he hadn't heard him. Then he gives him a look like a madman: the same terrible look of the boy many years before.*)

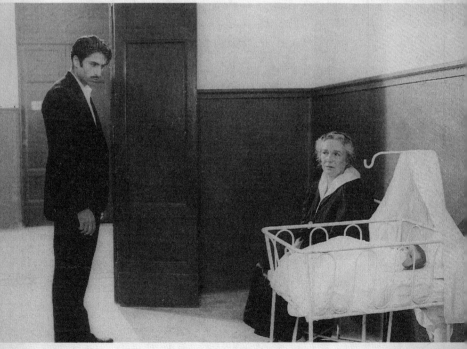

NICOLA: You really think you're something, don't you!
  (NICOLA *walks away down the corridor.*)

85. INT. BONANNO BROS OFFICE. DAY

NICOLA *is packing his things into a suitcase.* ANDREA *enters behind him. Without turning towards* ANDREA, NICOLA *speaks.*

NICOLA: Don't, I'm leaving.
  (ANDREA *starts to say something, but gives in to an infinite tired sadness.*)

ANDREA: It's your sorrow, I know, and I don't want to take it from you.

NICOLA: You are the lucky one, I don't want to end up being jealous of you.

ANDREA: It's not my fault!

NICOLA: But you're luckier, it's true, yes?

ANDREA: What are you talking about? You're not behaving like a brother.

NICOLA: What does 'brother' mean?

ANDREA: I don't know, but let us take care of you and your son!

NICOLA: (*His hatred returning*) I'm not leaving him with you.

ANDREA: Why not?

NICOLA: Not on your life. (*Beat.*) We're not equal any more.
Let's go get him.

ANDREA: Are you out of your mind? My wife is nursing him!
(*For a second* NICOLA *looks disconcerted. Then he recovers,
stubborn and unbending.*)

NICOLA: We are not equal any more.

86. EXT. STREET OUTSIDE THE STUDIO. DAY

The two brothers are walking. Suddenly, ANDREA *pushes* NICOLA.

ANDREA: Go by yourself. I don't want to see you ever again!

NICOLA: *You* don't? Imagine me!
(*They seem about to fight, as they did years ago over the silver
knife. But they remain still, locked in this unresolved conflict.*)

87. INT. ANDREA'S HOUSE. DAY

ANDREA *is outside, alone, staring out to sea. The camera pulls back
into the room where* MABEL *and* THOMPSON *are talking.*

THOMPSON: When does he plan to go back to work?

MABEL: I don't know. He tries . . . He draws and draws . . .
He's unhappy. He tears it all up . . . I try to encourage
him . . . I try to help.
(*She starts crying.*)

THOMPSON: And his brother Nicola?

MABEL: He entrusted the baby to Marga, our old friend. He's sailing
for Italy today. He decided to join the army . . . to go and fight.

88. EXT. BEACH. DAY

ANDREA *crashes the cymbals together.*

89. INT. PORT BAR. DAY

Over the sound of the cymbals NICOLA *is seen sitting alone at a table
in the bar. The camera moves past him to a glass of wine on the
table. Crash of cymbals. Close shot of* NICOLA'S *face, staring.*

90. EXT. BEACH. DAY

ANDREA *throws the cymbals into the sea.*

89

91. INT. PORT BAR. DAY

NICOLA's eyes are so concentrated they bulge: they want to make the glass move the way it did the other time. The glass doesn't budge. All at once, NICOLA brings his fist crashing down on the table, sending the glass crashing to the floor. The sound of guns firing and explosions.

92. EXT. ITALIAN BATTLEFIELD. DAY

The landscape is grey, milky. A Romanesque cathedral crowns a nearby hill. One, two, three mines explode. The field has been torn up by the battle that has raged there. It looks like an immobile desert, but suddenly dozens of Italian soldiers leap to their feet and start marching, leaping over their fallen comrades. Some don't get up again. One of these is the regiment's cameraman, hit by shrapnel from a mine. Beside him lies the abandoned camera. Another SOLDIER notices it and gives a shout.

SOLDIER: Lieutenant! The cameraman's dead!

(Close shot of the camera, lying on the ground. The LIEUTENANT picks up the camera, but doesn't know what to do with it.)

LIEUTENANT: (*Shouting*) Where's that soldier who was in
   America – what's his name? Hollywood.
   (*A soldier steps out of line and walks over to the* LIEUTENANT:
   NICOLA.)
   Hollywood?
NICOLA: Yessir.
   (*The* LIEUTENANT *shows him the camera.*)
LIEUTENANT: Do you know how to use this?
   (NICOLA *takes the camera and looks at it.*)
NICOLA: It wasn't my job. But I'll try.
   (*Another series of cannon shots sends the soldiers running off
   again, leaping, falling. They disappear from sight. Fade out.*)

93. EXT. ANOTHER WAR ZONE. DAY

*From the top of a hill in the war zone, a US military ambulance
appears. The United States has now entered the war, and the
ambulance is part of the Expedition Corps in Italy. Sitting next to
the driver is* ANDREA. *He is wearing the uniform of an American
soldier. The ambulance passes several Italian soldiers.* ANDREA
leans out of the window and questions them in Italian.
ANDREA: Where's the Tuscan battalion?
ITALIAN SOLDIER: Up ahead. Near the Cathedral of San Vito, I
   think.
   (*Dissolve to –*)

94. EXT. BATTLEFIELD. SUNSET

*The ambulance pulls to a stop in the middle of the deserted
battlefield. The soldiers take up their positions. Some dig new
trenches. A* SOLDIER *points to the Cathedral.*
SOLDIER: You're Italian, know what church that is?
ANDREA: I don't know what it's called, I'm not from around
   here. (*Looking at it*) But it's a splendid Romanesque!
   (*Close shot of the Cathedral. Suddenly the image dissolves into a
   vision of the Cathedral being built many centuries ago. From the
   next hill, suddenly, in a terrifying, silent surprise attack,
   Austrian assault troops pour over the plain with their bayonets
   unsheathed. They wash over the American soldiers like a black
   wave, bayoneting the soldiers who haven't even had time to react.*

The Austrians have disappeared into the approaching night.
ANDREA *and the other soldiers lie on the ground. Dissolve to:*
dawn. The same field, same Cathedral. The same framing. In
the spot where the Austrians disappeared, we hear the sound of
furious firing. A few instants later a scraggy little group of
Austrians appears, fleeing this way. Some are wounded. Now
and then they stop to fire behind them. They disappear over the
hill. A patrol from the Tuscan battalion is chasing them. Then it,
too, disappears and again the field is deserted. Only one Italian
soldier has stayed behind, bent over the unconscious body of an
American comrade: it is NICOLA *beside* ANDREA. NICOLA
stares at his brother's face. He feels like calling out to him,
shouting his name. ANDREA *isn't dead, but he's seriously*
wounded. NICOLA *grabs him under the arms to revive him. He*
lifts him up. ANDREA *regains consciousness with a moan.*
NICOLA *starts dragging him over the field, calling for help.*)

NICOLA: Lieutenant!!
(*His terrible cry of despair echoes over the field littered with*
corpses. He starts dragging his brother along again. Someone has
heard his shout and is running towards him. NICOLA *doesn't*
realize it's an enemy: an AUSTRIAN SOLDIER *who has got*
separated from his regiment and who is running like a fearful,
ferocious animal. NICOLA *doesn't have time to stand up. The*
AUSTRIAN, *terrified out of his wits to find him in the way, sticks*
him in the stomach with his bayonet. NICOLA *falls to the ground*
with a cry. The AUSTRIAN *is going to gouge him again, but*
ANDREA, *as though roused by* NICOLA's *cry or by brotherly*
instinct, grabs the enemy by the legs, knocks him down and stabs
him. Now NICOLA *and* ANDREA *drag themselves to one*
another's side and together try to help each other up. But they
haven't the strength to go on.)

95. EXT. BATTLEFIELD. NIGHT
The bodies of the soldiers lie abandoned on the field.

96. EXT. BATTLEFIELD. DAY
ANDREA *and* NICOLA, *mortally wounded, lie next to each other on*
the field.

ANDREA: I was sure I'd find you here.

NICOLA: I knew that the Americans had come.

(*Their voices echo over the deserted, scarred plain where the battle has raged. A shiver of death runs through both of them. They feel the need to say so many things. They want to tell each other that, now that they're together again, they want to live and make a fresh start. Instead,* NICOLA *just murmurs:*)

I hate so much to die, you know, Andrea.

(ANDREA'*s words come back to him like an echo.*)

ANDREA: I hate that our sons will never see our faces.

(*The two brothers lie on the battlefield, absorbed in this unbearable thought. The camera pans over the ground till it comes to a stop in front of the regiment's camera, lying abandoned amid the dead. The two brothers stare fixedly at the camera on the ground, while their eyes light up with the same thought.*)

I know what you're thinking, and I agree.

NICOLA: When they come by here they'll pick it up. This way our sons will know always what we look like.

(Cut to: close shot of the camera on its tripod. ANDREA *looks through the lens at* NICOLA. *He starts turning the crank. Close shot of* NICOLA's *face, as if through the lens of the camera. His face is bleeding and muddy.)*

ANDREA: Wipe your face off, Nicola. Do you want your son to see you like that?

*(*NICOLA *tries to take the mud and blood off his face.* ANDREA *shoots.)*

(Murmuring) Now, try to give him a smile.

NICOLA: I am smiling!

(Through the lens, NICOLA's *face appears. He think's he's smiling, but silent tears trickle from his eyes.* ANDREA *suddenly feels faint. For a second he loses consciousness. To keep from falling he grabs hold of the tripod under the camera.* NICOLA *supports him, panting hard. Cut to: close shot of* NICOLA *looking through the lens.* NICOLA *turns the crank.* ANDREA's *face now appears. He bows his head and brings his hands together on his chest. Then he raises them into the air, over his head, staring straight in front of him, in the blessing that*

belonged to his father, and his father's father before him . . .
Cut to: The façade of the Romanesque Cathedral which, with
all its wounds, rises up against the smoke-darkened sky, in a
silence sporadically broken by the sinister sounds of war.
Slowly, this image is transformed and the Romanesque façade
reappears in all its colours. Sunlight plays over its white, pink
and blue marble, over its pure lines, in the splendour of when it
was built many centuries ago. We're in the Middle Ages, and
teams of artisans are swarming over the scaffolding in their
colourful costumes. They follow the orders of the master builder,
who has the face of ANDREA's *and* NICOLA's *father. He has on*
the long red robe worn by the master builders of his day. Around
him move his seven sons. He is being hoisted up the front of the
Cathedral to where his two youngest sons, ANDREA *and*
NICOLA, *wearing short bright-coloured tunics, work together on*
a precious bas-relief. In the middle of it a white elephant
stands, raising his trunk in the air.)

96